THE HOUSE

Brian Parks is an American playwright whose work has been produced in New York City as well as in several cities across the U.S. The plays have also been produced internationally, in London, Edinburgh, Ireland, Adelaide, Heidelberg, Frankfurt, Berlin, Cologne, and Austria. His play *Americana Absurdum* helped launch the New York International Fringe Festival in 1997, where it also won the Best Writing Award. *Americana Absurdum* went on to win a Fringe First award at the 2000 Edinburgh Festival Fringe and became one of the first plays staged at London's Menier Chocolate Factory theatre. His other plays include *Goner, The Invitation, Imperial Fizz, American Poodle (Splayfoot), Suspicious Package, Out of the Way, The Professor, The House, Enterprise,* and *The Golfer.* Several of his plays – *Americana Absurdum, Goner, American Poodle (Splayfoot), Imperial Fizz, Enterprise* and *The House* – have appeared at the Edinburgh Festival Fringe, staged at Assembly venues. *Enterprise* won a Fringe First award in 2017. *Imperial Fizz* has been published by Josef Weinberger Plays, and *Enterprise* by Broadway Play Publishing. *The Invitation* has been published in the collection *Plays and Playwrights 2010*, by the New York Theater Experience, Inc.

"There is no American playwright more thoughtful – in an explosive and surreally comic way – than Brian Parks."
The Scotsman

"A refreshingly mischievous, inventive author."
The Times

Website: brianparksplaywright.com

THE HOUSE

by Brian Parks

JOSEF WEINBERGER PLAYS

LONDON

THE HOUSE
First published in 2018
by Josef Weinberger Ltd
12-14 Mortimer Street, London W1T 3JJ
www.josef-weinberger.com / plays@jwmail.co.uk

ISBN: 978 0 85676 378 6

THE HOUSE premiered on September 10, 2014, at the Kitchen Theatre Company in Ithaca, New York, with the following cast and creative contributors:

FISCHER .... Matthew Bretschneider

LINDSAY........................... Dana Berger

MARTYN .... Matthew Boston

SHANNY .... Elizabeth Meadows Rouse

Directed by Margarett Perry
Stage managed by Jennifer Schilansky
Scenic and lighting design by Tyler M. Perry
Costume design by Lisa Boquist
Sound design by Lesley Lisa Greene
Props by Danielle Bulajewski
Assistant direction by Jenni Kuhn

Kitchen Theatre Company:
Rachel Lampert, Artistic Director
Stephen Nunley, Managing Director

The author offers his special thanks to Margarett Perry, for her work on the premiere of the play and its subsequent productions.

Lights up hard on the living room. MARTYN *is standing with his arms outstretched, indicating the house. The sense that everyone has just entered from outside.*

MARTYN	There it is!
LINDSAY	It's great.
FISCHER	We're very excited.
SHANNY	You should be!
MARTYN	It's a wonderful house.
FISCHER	We love it.
SHANNY	You'll love it as much as we did.
LINDSAY	It's almost exactly what we were looking for.
FISCHER	We saw, what, thirty houses?
LINDSAY	More.
SHANNY	And then you saw ours.
FISCHER	And then we saw this one.
LINDSAY	We feel very lucky.
MARTYN	Good, good –
LINDSAY	It's a wonderful place.
MARTYN	They built them properly back then. Didn't just toss them up.
SHANNY	They cared about quality.
LINDSAY	You can see it.

FISCHER   The brickwork –

LINDSAY   Lovely.

MARTYN   Great curb appeal.

FISCHER   That's why we noticed it.

MARTYN   Best on the block.

FISCHER   The way the windows –

LINDSAY   From the street, the house almost looks like it's smiling.

SHANNY   It does, it does!

MARTYN   A great place to come home to every day.

SHANNY   Wonderful.

LINDSAY   (*Pointing to unseen fireplace.*) And the mantel –

FISCHER   We really wanted a house with a fireplace.

MARTYN   We use it all the time.

FISCHER   And we really like the bedroom layout upstairs.

LINDSAY   And the tub in the master bath.

SHANNY   A great place for a soak.

FISCHER   It's almost what we imagined for our new place.

SHANNY   It's comfy – a real home.

LINDSAY   And such a pretty neighborhood.

MARTYN   The best!

LINDSAY   All the trees.

MARTYN	They're oaks and Carpathian walnuts.
LINDSAY	"Such a friendly looking street," Fischer said.
MARTYN	He got that right.
SHANNY	We'll miss the neighbors terribly.
MARTYN	Good people.
SHANNY	The Bergmans next door –
MARTYN	Salt of the earth.
SHANNY	Great kids.
MARTYN	The Ungars down the block.
SHANNY	Retired, but always looking out for everyone.
MARTYN	The Helms across the street.
SHANNY	Lovely folks.
LINDSAY	Good neighbors are important.
FISCHER	People to count on if you're on vacation and there's some kind of explosion.
MARTYN	We'll miss them all a ton.
SHANNY	But with both the kids in college –
MARTYN	It was the right time to move on.
SHANNY	To this smaller condo we found.
MARTYN	It's just us now – a dentist, his wife, and their cat.
SHANNY	Some friends think we're moving too early, but we want to live the next part of our lives while we're still young enough to enjoy it.

MARTYN   Use the extra sale money for some travel.

SHANNY   To relax a little, finally.

MARTYN   And we don't want Sarah and Tommy thinking
                they can move back in after they graduate.

LINDSAY   It has a good foundation, says the inspector.

MARTYN   The furnace is only a year old.

FISCHER   We saw some brand-new places, but they felt
                wrong.

LINDSAY   Soulless.

FISCHER   This place felt just right.

SHANNY   It's made Martyn and I very happy.

MARTYN   I can still see the kids coming down the stairs
                on Christmas morning.

SHANNY   In their pajamas (*Makes wide-eyed look.*) with
                eyes like this.

LINDSAY   That's one of the reasons for our move.

FISCHER   Children.

LINDSAY   We wanted the right place to start a family.

FISCHER   Our current place is too small.

LINDSAY   Maybe okay for one kid –

FISCHER   But we'd like more than that.

LINDSAY   When we saw this place, we could already
                picture them running all around it.

FISCHER   Like they already lived there.

LINDSAY   We had to buy it for *them*.

SHANNY   They'll be grown before you know it.

MARTYN   One minute they're spitting up on your
               shoulder, the next throwing up from too many
               beers.

SHANNY   (*Snapping fingers.*) It goes like *that*.

MARTYN   And then your little baby is out there driving a
               car –

SHANNY   Reading novels –

MARTYN   And taking backpack trips through Muslim
               countries.

LINDSAY   (*Happily.*) Sounds great.

FISCHER   We're ready for all of it.

MARTYN   But at the center is always the house.

SHANNY   It's like another member of the family.

MARTYN   Which is why it was so important we sell it
               ourselves.

SHANNY   (*Good-naturedly.*) That and saving the broker's
               fee.

MARTYN   We didn't want to sell to just anyone. We
               wanted to *entrust* it to someone.

SHANNY   Right.

MARTYN   Almost like *marrying* it off.

SHANNY   You just want to *know*.

MARTYN   Exactly.

SHANNY   *Know* it's in good, loving hands.

MARTYN   Can't trust a real estate broker with that.

SHANNY   Friends of ours sold their house and the new owners knocked it down to build a bigger place.

MARTYN   Beautiful 1920s Tudor.

SHANNY   Leaded windows, gorgeous library.

MARTYN   They put their heart and soul into it.

SHANNY   (*Making sweeping, wrecking-ball gesture.*) Then *boom*.

MARTYN   The broker said they were good people.

SHANNY   Proving yet again how horrible real estate brokers are.

MARTYN   An extremely low life form.

SHANNY   Like a silverfish.

MARTYN   Liars, all of 'em.

SHANNY   Try looking in their eyes.

MARTYN   You can't.

SHANNY   Always jittering this way and that.

MARTYN   And they walk too fast.

SHANNY   Trying to get away from their guilt.

MARTYN   That's why real estate brokers are always covered in rashes.

SHANNY   From the guilt!

FISCHER   My cousin is a real-estate broker.

(*An awkward pause.*)

FISCHER   He's a dick.

                 (*Relief from* MARTYN *and* SHANNY.)

LINDSAY   That's why we didn't use him.

FISCHER   Went with that new guy instead.

LINDSAY   And since I'm an attorney, the tricky parts I understand anyway.

SHANNY   Well, you were our favorite people who came to see it.

FISCHER   Thanks.

MARTYN   Your bid was actually *lower* than another couple's.

LINDSAY   Really?

SHANNY   They were nice, but we liked you even better.

MARTYN   You can tell these things.

SHANNY   Yep.

MARTYN   Even though we only met you on your house tours –

SHANNY   You were the couple we could see living here.

MARTYN   We could really see the enthusiasm in your eyes.

SHANNY   They were *glowing*.

MARTYN   So giving up the extra sale money –

SHANNY   Seemed right rather than wrong.

LINDSAY   We're very flattered.

FISCHER   So generous of you.

MARTYN   Not at all.

SHANNY   Because we got what *we* wanted by having *you* take over.

LINDSAY   Well, thank you, really.

MARTYN   But boy, I was pretty nervous just now signing all those sale documents back at that office.

LINDSAY   Closings are always stressful.

MARTYN   And when I had that pen in my hand –

FISCHER   Can't blame you for hesitating there a bit.

MARTYN   Selling didn't seem quite real till then. With everyone gathered around, and all the contracts on the table. And so much money involved. It's amazing you could pay for the house in cash.

LINDSAY   A family tradition that got drilled into me.

FISCHER   Plus we got a great price on the old place.

LINDSAY   Our jobs pay well, along with some inheritance and a lot of savings.

FISCHER   Fewer closing fees and no mortgage interest.

LINDSAY   It's just simpler and more certain.

FISCHER   And this way we really own it *all* ourselves.

LINDSAY   No matter what.

MARTYN   Well, thanks so much for letting us stay the extra ten weeks.

SHANNY   Without charging us anything.

LINDSAY   Of course.

MARTYN   This all happened a little faster than we thought.

FISCHER   Least we could do for the nice price.

MARTYN   So helpful with our move, after so long here.

SHANNY   It's going to take a while to get it all sorted out and packed up. It'll be strange to think we're staying in someone else's house.

MARTYN   When it looks just the same.

SHANNY   Hard to believe this is actually happening.

MARTYN   Yep.

SHANNY   (*Looking around at the house.*) It's been so long –

MARTYN   A long time.

SHANNY   The house . . .

MARTYN   I know . . .

SHANNY   (*Tearing up a bit.*) And now . . .

MARTYN   (*To* FISCHER and LINDSAY) It's the right choice for us.

SHANNY   It is . . .

MARTYN   Just a little hard.

SHANNY   Yes.

MARTYN   You'll see one day.

FISCHER   (*Reassuring.*) Oh, I'm sure.

MARTYN   After so much has happened in your life in one place. (*Pause.*) Okay, the keys!

(MARTYN *pulls out a set of keys and holds them up in the air between the two couples.*)

MARTYN   (*Somewhat more dramatically this time.*) The keys.

SHANNY   We really wanted to give them to you *here*.

MARTYN   The right place to do it.

SHANNY   In the house.

LINDSAY   A perfect plan!

                (*Each couple looks at the keys dangling and shining in the air. Then* LINDSAY *slowly reaches out to take them from* MARTYN. MARTYN, *so attached to his home, can't quite let go of them,* LINDSAY *tugging at them. Then he lets go. Then* MARTYN *hugs* SHANNY, FISCHER *hugs* LINDSAY. *Then* MARTYN *speaks to break the mood.*)

MARTYN   (*Enthusiastically.*) And now – the drinks!

SHANNY   The drinks!

FISCHER   The drinks!

MARTYN   Back in a flash.

FISCHER   Need some help with that?

MARTYN   No, no, relax – I'm good.

                (MARTYN *exits to kitchen.*)

LINDSAY   (*Admiring the keys in her hand.*) Wow, look at these.

SHANNY   We made a special set up new. The big round one is the front door, and the square one is the door from the garage. That third one we forget, but we made a copy of it anyway.

FISCHER	Well, thank you.
LINDSAY	(*Passing keys to* FISCHER) The keys to our new house.
FISCHER	(*Nervously-excitedly shaking keys.*) They rattle.
SHANNY	Yep, they're keys. Martyn also made up a folder of things, the garage door company and other local numbers you'll need. A map of the neighbors' houses, saying who's who.
LINDSAY	It's going to be great here.
FISCHER	Not sure I've ever been this excited.
LINDSAY	Only our wedding day.
FISCHER	That was more just really nervous.
SHANNY	Houses and marriages – they're both big commitments.
LINDSAY	And quite alike in lots of ways.
SHANNY	You hope both last a long time.
LINDSAY	Right!
SHANNY	They both take work.
LINDSAY	Both keep you warm in the winter.
SHANNY	Both get more character with age.
FISCHER	Both come with big water bills.
	(*Pause.* LINDSAY *and* SHANNY *both a little confused.*)
FISCHER	Lindsay loves her baths.
LINDSAY	Guilty.

FISCHER   And uses the toilet a *lot*.

LINDSAY   Well, we can't wait to move in and get all set up.

FISCHER   We're already done picking out some paint
                colors.

SHANNY   Paint?

LINDSAY   Oh, nothing much.

FISCHER   A few rooms.

LINDSAY   Just some touches.

FISCHER   I have a thing for red.

LINDSAY   He's always got to have a few rooms red.

FISCHER   A warm red –

LINDSAY   He thinks it's cozy.

FISCHER   It is –

LINDSAY   So I let him get away with it.

FISCHER   Not like *murdered-by-Serbians* red.

SHANNY   (*Good-naturedly.*) Well, lord knows the place
                could use a few touch-ups.

LINDSAY   To make a beautiful house even better.

                (MARTYN *re-enters with the drinks.*)

MARTYN   Here we go!

FISCHER   Great, great.

MARTYN   (*Handing out drinks.*) Scotches for Fischer and
                myself.

FISCHER   Thank you.

MARTYN   (*Handing wine to* LINDSAY *and* SHANNY.) And some sauvignon blanc for the ladies. I picked a white since red is such an icky color.

                    (*An awkward pause.*)

MARTYN   (*Sensing something wrong.*) Would you like a cab instead?

LINDSAY   No, no – this is fine.

MARTYN   Good, good.

LINDSAY   Thank you very much.

MARTYN   Well, then – a toast!

SHANNY   Finally!

MARTYN   To celebrate such an important day! To Fischer and Lindsay – may they love this house as much as our family has.

LINDSAY   (*Toasting.*) And to Martyn and Shanny, for letting us be the ones to buy the house that's meant the world to them.

FISCHER   At a discount!

SHANNY   Cheers!

                    (*They all clink glasses and drink from their drinks. Then* SHANNY *speaks, addressing* LINDSAY *and* FISCHER.)

SHANNY   You know, we moved in here with a lot of dreams. But they mostly all came true. To raise a happy, healthy family. To make a real home. To have a wonderful life. And we've had that here. We were a little lucky, I suppose, but I think this house had a lot to do with it. Sounds funny, but I think it actually cared about us. You may not know what I mean, but you will. After you've lived here a while. Now it's time for it to take care of your family. However many kids you have running up and down those dang stairs. Making their favorite dinners in the kitchen. Picking all their crap up off the floor. Your own cat climbing on everything. We're making the house sad by leaving, I think. But the time is right. We'll miss it like . . . well, we'll miss it. (*Pause.*) Just don't let your husband do any wiring by himself.

LINDSAY   We'll love it.

MARTYN   You will, you will!

FISCHER   The whole area.

MARTYN   There are a lot of great restaurants in town.

LINDSAY   Yes, we noticed.

MARTYN   And boutiques.

SHANNY   You like boutiques?

LINDSAY   Love boutiques.

MARTYN   Got boutiques.

SHANNY   Dress boutiques.

MARTYN   Tie boutiques.

SHANNY   Rug boutiques.

FISCHER   Hat boutiques?

MARTYN   Candle boutiques.

LINDSAY   Holiday boutiques?

SHANNY   Jewelry boutiques.

LINDSAY ·   (*To* FISCHER, *impressed.*) Nice boutiques.

MARTYN   We got a good public golf course.

FISCHER   Great!

MARTYN   You play?

FISCHER   All my life.

MARTYN   Golf is the best!

FISCHER   The fresh air and green grass.

MARTYN   Beautiful landscapes where swearing is
                perfectly acceptable.

SHANNY   And there's a nice swim club. Our son Tommy
                was a life guard there.

MARTYN   Helped save an old lady once.

SHANNY   (*To* MARTYN.) She was my age.

MARTYN   She cramped up and started to go under –

SHANNY   Tommy dived right in and pulled her out.

MARTYN   Saved her life.

SHANNY   She bought him a bike after.

MARTYN   A very sweet old lady.

SHANNY   The town also has excellent services.

LINDSAY   That's what we've heard.

SHANNY   Trash pick-up is like clockwork.

MARTYN   And they take zoning very seriously.

SHANNY	The utility people have always been helpful.
MARTYN	(*To* LINDSAY.) Plus the handsome mailman.
SHANNY	Martyn –
MARTYN	He's quite good-looking.
SHANNY	Not again, Martyn.
MARTYN	I tease her about their affair.
SHANNY	There's no affair.
MARTYN	(*Teasing.*) None.
SHANNY	He's a nice man.
MARTYN	And handsome.
SHANNY	This is Martyn's little joke.
MARTYN	(*Semi-joking.*) Who could resist a man who smells like catalogues?
SHANNY	You're the one with his hands in other women's mouths all day –
MARTYN	Just doing my job.
SHANNY	I hope so.
MARTYN	(*A little wistfully.*) The pretty ones are always the grinders.
FISCHER	(*Gazing around at the house.*) You know, this place is sort of like the house I grew up in.
MARTYN	Really?
FISCHER	Not exactly. But our living room was like this, and the front door area. And the kitchen was in basically the same place.

MARTYN	You'll really feel at home, then.
FISCHER	Kind of strange now that I think about it.
SHANNY	I suppose it's not surprising to find a place that feels familiar.
LINDSAY	Wouldn't want it to be exactly the same, though.
FISCHER	That would be sort of weird.
LINDSAY	Move in and start putting up your old rock posters.
SHANNY	Wouldn't be healthy.
MARTYN	Nope.
SHANNY	If it starts happening, talk to a psychologist.
FISCHER	Oh, it won't –
MARTYN	They can be very helpful.
FISCHER	I'm sure.
MARTYN	Perk you right up.
SHANNY	No shame in it.
MARTYN	Not these days.
SHANNY	Used to be.
MARTYN	For sure.
SHANNY	Back then, if people heard you went to a psychologist, they'd look at you kind of funny.
MARTYN	But it's different now. So don't worry if you need to see one.
FISCHER	I won't need to.

MARTYN	There are a couple psychologists who work in my office building. I run into their patients in the hall. The patients look *completely* normal.
FISCHER	Good.
MARTYN	Though I make sure to be extra polite, just in case.
FISCHER	(*Trying to change the topic.*) This location seems very convenient.
SHANNY	There's a big supermarket five minutes away.
FISCHER	Great.
SHANNY	Big aisles, good deli counter. The checkout girls work real fast. So fast they sometimes forget to scan something and you get it for free.
LINDSAY	You don't let them know?
SHANNY	Heck, no – I'm a valued customer.
FISCHER	Glad it's so close.
SHANNY	It's got a pharmacy, but we use the one over on the main road instead. Been there forever.
MARTYN	Good people.
SHANNY	The best. You can trust them. Not to go talking. Think of some of the things people get prescriptions for.
	(*A sort of awkward pause as everyone considers this idea.*)
LINDSAY	You said last time you were happy with the schools.
MARTYN	They're excellent.

SHANNY   Experienced faculty.

MARTYN   Kids getting into top colleges.

SHANNY   There's a private academy in town, but the
                tuition there –

MARTYN   Huge!

SHANNY   And it's full of spoiled rich kids. It has a horse
                club. Some of the girls wear their riding get-ups
                around town as a show-off thing. Who raises
                kids that way? Who raises kids to act superior in
                a helmet?

FISCHER   I think we'll be sticking to the public schools.

LINDSAY   I want our kids to have good teachers, like I did.

FISCHER   I had a great math and geometry teacher in high
                school.

MARTYN   Geometry's tough.

FISCHER   See, he made it completely easy. Had a big
                beard. Wore the same plaid shirt every day. "Mr
                Libbett," he'd say to me, "Mr Libbett, you draw
                a wonderful dodecagon!"

                (FISCHER *gestures and smiles proudly. The others
                look at him somewhat mystified.*)

FISCHER   (*Explaining, after pause.*) It's a twelve-sided
                polygon.

                (*A pause, still some mystery.*)

FISCHER   Polygons are . . . They can walk to the schools,
                right?

SHANNY   Or bike.

LINDSAY   Sounds like this location has everything.

FISCHER   Property taxes are a shade high.

LINDSAY   They're fine.

MARTYN   Think of it as everyone chipping in a little extra
                   to keep home values up.

SHANNY   And for the parks and tennis courts and police.

MARTYN   It's very safe.

SHANNY   Almost no crime.

MARTYN   Can't think of the last one.

SHANNY   Ages.

MARTYN   Maybe some shoplifting.

LINDSAY   That's anyplace.

SHANNY   Tom Polonich stole his company's pension fund.

MARTYN   (*Remembering.*) Oh, there was that.

SHANNY   Never liked him.

MARTYN   Nope.

SHANNY   He had a look –

MARTYN   Yep.

SHANNY   An odd one –

MARTYN   Oh, yeah.

SHANNY   Whenever you saw him.

MARTYN   Always.

SHANNY	Then we learned.
MARTYN	It was a look that said, "I'm stealing a pension fund."
LINDSAY	Fischer researched it, and they said the neighborhood is very safe.
FISCHER	And we're glad the neighbors sound nice.
MARTYN	You don't want bad neighbors.
FISCHER	We got a few doozies at our current place. Mr 6 a.m. Lawnmower Man.
LINDSAY	Twice a week!
FISCHER	The guy with the talking car alarm.
LINDSAY	(*In robot voice.*) "You are too close to this unwashed vehicle."
FISCHER	Mr White Boy Rapper next door.
LINDSAY	Oh, Christ.
FISCHER	Unbearable.
LINDSAY	Every day in the backyard.
FISCHER	How many times do you need to hear someone rhyme the word "pussy"?
MARTYN	(*After brief awkwardness.*) And churches – all kinds of churches in the neighborhood. What religion are you?
LINDSAY	Well, I'm not sure we're anything, exactly.
MARTYN	Nothing?
SHANNY	Everybody's something.

FISCHER   Not so much for us.

SHANNY   Your families must have been something.

FISCHER   Well, there were some Catholics back in there.

LINDSAY   A Presbyterian or two.

MARTYN   Presbyterians are alright.

LINDSAY   My grandfather was Lutheran.

FISCHER   Nobody Jewish.

LINDSAY   Nope.

FISCHER   I didn't mean that to sound strange.

MARTYN   Nothing wrong with Jewishness.

FISCHER   Right.

SHANNY   Those people have been through a lot.

FISCHER   You bet.

MARTYN   History's been tough on 'em.

LINDSAY   Even today people are hard on them.

FISCHER   Weird.

MARTYN   Must be a real struggle.

LINDSAY   I'll say.

MARTYN   All the time. Jewishness can be a real cross to bear.

SHANNY   We're Episcopalians ourselves.

MARTYN   The church is just two blocks away.

SHANNY	Big congregation.
FISCHER	What do Episcopalians believe?
MARTYN	Well . . . quite a lot.
FISCHER	Like what?
MARTYN	In God, of course – that's pretty basic.
SHANNY	And Jesus.
MARTYN	Yep, Jesus is up there.
LINDSAY	He's in most religions.
FISCHER	What are the different parts?
SHANNY	Different parts?
FISCHER	That nobody else has.
MARTYN	(*Thinking.*) Well, let's see. Everybody has crucifixion.
SHANNY	Yep.
MARTYN	The prayers.
SHANNY	Right.
MARTYN	(*Realizing a difference.*) We have a coat of arms!
SHANNY	It's a good religion.
MARTYN	Nothing too extreme about it.
SHANNY	Nope.
MARTYN	No one's cutting off your hands or making you wear heavy coats in hot weather.
SHANNY	So you're atheists?

LINDSAY   Maybe more agnostic, I suppose.

MARTYN   (*Wanting to be helpful.*) Try some Episcopalianism.

SHANNY   You can walk to it! (*Indicating empty glass.*) Ah, my drink is gone.

MARTYN   Then Doctor Martyn prescribes another.

SHANNY   No, that's fine, I –

MARTYN   Special occasion!

                (MARTYN *exits*.)

SHANNY   It's going to be strange waking up in a different bedroom after all these years.

FISCHER   I imagine.

SHANNY   But it'll be good to have less house to worry about. The condo association takes care of everything at our new place. *They* mow the lawn. *They* shovel the driveway. Never again do I have to worry about an attic full of bees.

LINDSAY   Does the attic –

SHANNY   *They* rake the leaves and haul the trash down to the curb.

FISCHER   Sounds like a great place.

SHANNY   And it's not all full of old folks. I like the sound of birds, not respirators.

                (MARTYN *returns carrying a bottle of scotch, a bottle of white wine, and a shallow bowl overloaded with nuts*.)

MARTYN   And we're back!

FISCHER   Looks like a party.

MARTYN	It *is* a party. (*To* SHANNY *re. wine.*) More for you. (*To* FISCHER *and* LINDSAY *re. scotch and wine.*) And more for you. (*Holding up the bowl of nuts.*) And I brought some of our favorite nuts.
SHANNY	Great!
LINDSAY	Thank you.
	(MARTYN *turns to* LINDSAY *to say "You're welcome"* –)
MARTYN	You're welcome –
	(*But his arm turns too quickly, and the nuts go flying out of the shallow bowl onto both the floor and* LINDSAY, *who is seated. Many land in her lap on her skirt.*)
LINDSAY	Oh!
MARTYN	Oh, Jesus –
SHANNY	Martyn!
MARTYN	Apologies! I –
SHANNY	They're everywhere –
	(MARTYN *gets down on his knees and starts picking up nuts.*)
MARTYN	Yikes, so sorry about that –
LINDSAY	Oh – no, it's fine –
SHANNY	(*Re.* MARTYN.) So clumsy sometimes –
FISCHER	No worries, Martyn –
MARTYN	(*Re. the scattered nuts.*) I'll just get these –

(MARTYN *starts picking the nuts off of*
LINDSAY'S *lap,* LINDSAY *with a very awkward /
uncomfortable look on her face.*)

SHANNY   Are your clothes okay?

LINDSAY   I do like nuts normally.

MARTYN   Oh, good, good –

FISCHER   We both do.

LINDSAY   These were probably nice ones.

SHANNY   We special-order them –

MARTYN   I can go back and get some more –

LINDSAY   (*Firmly.*) No, really – just the wine is good.

MARTYN   (*To* FISCHER, *trying to make conversation while
              on the floor picking up rest of nuts.*) So, ah,
              you're in finance, right?

FISCHER   Yep.

SHANNY   Those people don't have the greatest reputation
              these days.

MARTYN   From what you see in the papers.

FISCHER   Well, that's complicated. People like to criticize
              the financial world, but it's what makes things
              run. (*To* MARTYN.) Makes your dental tools and
              X-ray machines. (*To* SHANNY.) Gets your big
              refrigerator manufactured and shipped across
              country. None of that can happen without deals
              and money flow. We don't build the cars, but
              without us there aren't going to be any cars. No
              toothbrush or toothpaste companies. People
              would have to clean their teeth with old rags
              and turpentine.

SHANNY   (*Incorrectly.*) Like in Australia.

MARTYN   (*To* LINDSAY.) And you're at Huber and Howe,
                  right?

FISCHER   (*Proudly, re.* LINDSAY.) A partner someday!

LINDSAY   Someday.

MARTYN   I have a patient from that law firm.

LINDSAY   Oh, really – who?

MARTYN   (*Good-naturedly.*) Confidential.

SHANNY   Oh, you can say.

MARTYN   Nope, nope – I took an oath.

LINDSAY   Dentists have oaths?

MARTYN   (*Proudly.*) Just like MDs do.

LINDSAY   What's it called?

MARTYN   (*After brief pause.*) I . . . I don't remember.

FISCHER   Maybe it's named for a famous Greek dentist.

SHANNY   (*Pondering.*) Famous Greek dentist . . .

                  (*Everyone pauses to see if they can think of who
                  that could be. But to no avail.*)

FISCHER   Had you wanted to be a doctor instead?

MARTYN   Nope, always a dentist.

FISCHER   (*Good-naturedly.*) Oh, that's good. I've heard
                  most dentists wanted to be doctors but couldn't
                  get into medical school.

MARTYN   (*Laughing it off.*) Oh, maybe a few.

FISCHER   It's where dentists' high rate of suicide comes
                 from.

LINDSAY   (*To* FISCHER.) Plenty of people dream of being
                 dentists, dear.

FISCHER   Oh, I suppose, sure.

LINDSAY   (*Good-naturedly.*) Plus the elf on that Christmas
                 TV show.

SHANNY   Right!

FISCHER   Sure, yep! (*Brief pause.*) Though he was an elf.

MARTYN   It's a good job for meeting nice people.

FISCHER   That's better than mine.

LINDSAY   Some of his coworkers are not the friendliest.

FISCHER   Lawyers are worse.

LINDSAY   Nope.

FISCHER   Oh, c'mon – Joe Bergeron?

LINDSAY   (*Conceding.*) There is him.

FISCHER   (*To* MARTYN *and* SHANNY.) Whatever you do, he
                 has to top it. Get a new coat, he gets a nicer
                 one. Read a good book, he's read a better one.
                 Tell a joke, he's got a funnier one that involves
                 even more pygmies.

LINDSAY   (*To* MARTYN *and* SHANNY.) So it sounds like you
                 indeed work with the nicer people.

SHANNY   And not all dentists care as much as Martyn.

MARTYN   Pick carefully if you want a local one when you
                 move in.

SHANNY   Why, you should see Martyn!

MARTYN   Sure, sure!

SHANNY   He'd love to have you as new patients.

MARTYN   (*Enthusiastically.*) Can always make room.

LINDSAY   We already have one on our side of the city –

FISCHER   Dr McCarty.

SHANNY   That'll be a long drive from this house.

MARTYN   Forty minutes.

SHANNY   Martyn's just a few miles.

MARTYN   (*Eyeing* LINDSAY *and* FISCHER'S *teeth.*) Your
                teeth look pretty good, but if there was an
                emergency –

SHANNY   Then somebody closer –

LINDSAY   We've been pretty happy with our guy.

MARTYN   Oh, that's good, yes. Just if you're looking for
                someone once you're here.

FISCHER   A good option.

MARTYN   Right, right.

FISCHER   Something to definitely keep in mind.

MARTYN   Please do.

LINDSAY   We will.

MARTYN   If you stop liking him, or the drive.

FISCHER   Sure thing.

MARTYN   Good, good.

                (*An awkward pause in the conversation, till*
                SHANNY *speaks.*)

SHANNY   (*To* MARTYN, *suddenly remembering.*) Oh – they
                say they might paint a different color.

MARTYN   Really?

LINDSAY   (*Good-naturedly.*) Just some things here and
                there.

MARTYN   (*Good-naturedly.*) Well, I . . . I guess if they're
                the new owners.

LINDSAY   You might like it.

MARTYN   It's pretty good colors now. Might move in and
                find you kinda like it this way.

LINDSAY   We're going to do it before we move all the
                stuff in.

MARTYN   Oh, well, I see, I see. I suppose that's easier.

LINDSAY   I'm sorry – we're seeming overeager. It's just we
                love it so much, we can't wait to live here.

SHANNY   Of course, of course.

MARTYN   We were pretty excited to move in ourselves.

SHANNY   Incredibly.

MARTYN   Had to fix a few things ourselves. Make a few
                changes here and there.

SHANNY   But it ended up being perfect for us.

MARTYN   A real home.

SHANNY   Plus all the wonderful detail.

MARTYN	The moldings, the wainscoting in the kitchen –
SHANNY	I've always loved the roses pattern in the parquet in the dining room.
LINDSAY	Oh, I didn't notice that.
MARTYN	Beautiful detail.
SHANNY	(*To* LINDSAY.) I'll show you!
LINDSAY	Sure!
	(SHANNY *and* LINDSAY *exit.*)
MARTYN	The place is full of things like that.
FISCHER	Yes, I saw a lot of them last time.
MARTYN	The den is great for football in the fall.
FISCHER	Looks it.
MARTYN	It's cozy. Nothing beats sitting in that den with a beer and the game on. You a fan?
FISCHER	So-so.
MARTYN	I love it.
FISCHER	I like basketball.
MARTYN	Pro or college?
FISCHER	Both.
MARTYN	Doesn't quite do it for me.
FISCHER	No?
MARTYN	(*Bothered by the sound.*) Squeaky shoes.
FISCHER	Great athletes, though.

MARTYN   Oh, sure.

FISCHER   The amazing ways they move when taking a
              shot, it's almost balletic.

MARTYN   See, I don't like ballet either.

FISCHER   Well, ballet itself, me neither.

MARTYN   (*Dismissively.*) Swans.

FISCHER   No swans in basketball.

MARTYN   Thank God there!

FISCHER   There should be a ballet about sports cars.

MARTYN   I'd go to that.

FISCHER   Or World War Two.

MARTYN   Right!

FISCHER   Pearl Harbor.

MARTYN   Sure! (*Considering the idea.*) Someone would
              have to dance as an aircraft carrier.

FISCHER   Maybe they teach that in ballet school.

MARTYN   See, I wouldn't know.

              (MARTYN *indicates* FISCHER's *drink.*)

MARTYN   You okay there?

FISCHER   Ah – yes, fine.

MARTYN   It's too bad for people who can't drink.

FISCHER   Yep.

MARTYN   A nice scotch or a glass of wine – just a great
              part of life.

FISCHER   Within reason.

MARTYN   Oh, sure, sure.

FISCHER   Can't go overdoing it all the time.

MARTYN   Nope.

FISCHER   Though a lot of alcoholism is actually
              biological.

MARTYN   (*Making drinking motion.*) Because you have to
              use your arm to do it.

FISCHER   I mean chemical, on the inside.

MARTYN   Right, right.

FISCHER   (*Points to his head.*) Combines wrong, then
              ruins their life.

MARTYN   Tragic.

FISCHER   (*Making "going downhill" gesture.*) Then it's
              just . . .

MARTYN   (*Agreeing.*) At least they get to enjoy themselves
              in the process.

              (*Another pause. Then* FISCHER *speaks.*)

FISCHER   (*Looking around.*) Twenty years here, eh?

MARTYN   Goes by faster than you think.

FISCHER   I wonder what me and Lindsay's life will be like
              in twenty years.

MARTYN   I'm guessing great.

FISCHER   Hope so!

MARTYN   More wrinkles, though.

FISCHER   Yeah.

MARTYN   Go a little gray.

FISCHER   Happens.

MARTYN   Aches and pains.

FISCHER   Got them already.

MARTYN   Your butts will get kinda flabby.

FISCHER   Our butts?

MARTYN   Just nature.

FISCHER   I suppose.

MARTYN   If it's already a problem, then it's nothing you
                 even have to worry about.

FISCHER   I guess we'll see.

MARTYN   Mine started going about ten years ago. Shanny's
                 – well, I'm too much of a gentleman to say.

FISCHER   No worries.

MARTYN   Time just kind of catches up with you. You lose
                 things, and people. But in return you get – well,
                 wisdom.

FISCHER   I'm sure.

MARTYN   Can I offer some?

FISCHER   All yours.

MARTYN	We men – we're protectors. That might sound corny in this day and age, but it's still true. Protecting Shanny, the kids – it's our job. Buying this house, in this good neighborhood, it's all part of your job to protect Lindsay – even though she's a lawyer and probably great at suing people. But never apologize for that role as protector. It's what I did here. It's not a fashionable idea these days. These days people want men to more like women. But women already exist, so what's the point of that, huh? No, protecting family is just in our DNA, like our eye color and whiskers and love of pretzels. It's why we're still in charge of the fireplace. *Andirons!* It's just what it means to be men.
FISCHER	(*After pause.*) Okay.
	(SHANNY *and* LINDSAY *re-enter.*)
SHANNY	I also showed her the doorframe with all the height marks for everyone.
MARTYN	The heights!
FISCHER	My family did the same thing growing up!
LINDSAY	Mine too!
SHANNY	We made a new mark every year on the kids' birthdays.
FISCHER	Right, right!
SHANNY	A lot of marks on there now.
MARTYN	So much history.
SHANNY	That all happened *here.*
MARTYN	Yep.

SHANNY	So many memories occurring between those height marks on the doorframe.
FISCHER	(*Looking around at the house and then at* LINDSAY.) Someday we'll have our own memories about this house.
LINDSAY	(*Realizing.*) We will.
FISCHER	Someday Lindsay and I will sit right here like you guys and talk about all the things that happened here. All the things with *our* family. And you know they'll all be good ones, because they're going to happen *here*. The memories we'll have twenty or twenty-five years from now.
SHANNY	(*Half-joking.*) We'll be dead then.
LINDSAY	(*Good-naturedly and reassuring.*) No.
FISCHER	Maybe! You never know. But that's also why you want a good house to count on. This will really be that place.
LINDSAY	(*Suddenly remembering.*) Oh, give them the present.
FISCHER	Right – of course!
	(FISCHER *retrieves a small gift bag they brought in when arriving and set down.*)
LINDSAY	We wanted to give you a little thank you.
MARTYN	Oh, not necessary.
FISCHER	For treating us so well.
	(FISCHER *hands the gift bag to* SHANNY, *who removes a fist-sized, abstract object from it.*)
MARTYN	You shouldn't have.

LINDSAY	A small token of our appreciation.
FISCHER	For picking us for the place.
MARTYN	Really, we're thrilled it was you.
	(SHANNY *does not know what the object is.*)
MARTYN	(*Hiding his own puzzlement.*) Well, look at that.
SHANNY	It's very nice.
	(SHANNY *hands the object to* MARTYN, *who begins examining it.*)
MARTYN	Yes, thank you.
LINDSAY	Of course.
MARTYN	That's great. Oh, look – it's engraved: "To the Redmonds, With Our Forever Thanks."
SHANNY	So sweet.
MARTYN	(*A brief pause as he looks at it, puzzled, then he speaks.*) What is it?
FISCHER	A paperweight.
MARTYN	Oh, of course!
SHANNY	Right, right!
FISCHER	(*To* MARTYN.) You can use it on a stack of papers at work.
MARTYN	Dentist offices can get windy.
FISCHER	You're all set then.
MARTYN	But we didn't get you anything.
LINDSAY	Oh, the house is enough.

SHANNY	We should have.
MARTYN	Over time, we've probably received more gifts than we've given.
SHANNY	A little embarrassing.
MARTYN	It is, it is. Though I guess the good part is we come out ahead.

(LINDSAY *has drifted to a set of family photos on a nearby shelf or table.*)

LINDSAY	These are your children here?
MARTYN	Yep – as kids and now.
LINDSAY	(*Indicating a photo.*) This is your daughter Sarah?
MARTYN	Taken last year at college.
LINDSAY	That is wonderful.
MARTYN	Yep.
LINDSAY	(*Looking at photo.*) That is *so inspiring*.
SHANNY	How so?
LINDSAY	That she could go to college despite having Down's Syndrome.

(*Awkward pause.*)

SHANNY	She doesn't.
LINDSAY	Oh.
MARTYN	(*Trying to find something to break the awkward moment.*) We think she's a lesbian.
FISCHER	That's better than Down's Syndrome!

LINDSAY   (*Very embarrassed.*) Could I have another wine?

SHANNY   Help yourself.

LINDSAY   I'm sorry I misunderstood.

MARTYN   Oh, no worries.

LINDSAY   I didn't mean that to sound –

MARTYN   No problem.

LINDSAY   The picture is just –

SHANNY   Just what?

LINDSAY   Just a little – you know.

SHANNY   A little . . . ?

LINDSAY   Retard . . . esque.

SHANNY   (*Trying to be good-natured, though a little put off.*) She's completely normal, count our blessings.

FISCHER   It's probably just the lighting in the shot.

LINDSAY   I'm sorry.

MARTYN   No harm meant.

SHANNY   Of course not.

FISCHER   (*Trying to be constructive.*) Next time, though, I'd use a new photographer.

LINDSAY   (*Indicating another photo, trying to recover.*) This other one is nice.

MARTYN   (*Trying to help things recover.*) That's me and Shanny the week of our engagement.

SHANNY   We met at the country fair.

LINDSAY   Were you displaying piglets?

MARTYN   No, no – I was there for the rides, me and two
                buddies.

SHANNY   I was there with two girlfriends –

MARTYN   But you could only fit two people in a
                rollercoaster car.

SHANNY   So Martyn and I ended up sharing one.

MARTYN   The carnie just sat us together.

FISCHER   Sounds like a movie!

SHANNY   (*Eager to know.*) Which one?

FISCHER   (*A little flustered.*) I'm not sure.

MARTYN   And now all those years later, here we are.

SHANNY   With a houseful of stuff to move. Where do we
                even start?

MARTYN   The condo is smaller –

SHANNY   Can't all go.

FISCHER   We're already fighting about what to move or
                throw out.

LINDSAY   Oh, yeah.

FISCHER   If you have to think twice about it, I say toss it.

LINDSAY   Well –

FISCHER   We both know a lot of it's crap. (*Points out
                a lamp in the room.*) She'd want to keep that
                lamp, for example.

SHANNY	We like that lamp.
FISCHER	(*Trying to apologize.*) I mean *our* version of a crappy lamp.
SHANNY	It was my mother's –
LINDSAY	She died?
MARTYN	Inoperable tumor.
LINDSAY	I'm sorry –
MARTYN	(*To* FISCHER, *gesturing with his hands.*) Size of a guinea pig.
SHANNY	Martyn –
MARTYN	Could've sold it to a pet shop.
LINDSAY	(*Being extra-nice to make up for lamp comment.*) The death of a parent – so difficult.
FISCHER	Our parents are all still alive.
MARTYN	That's great.
FISCHER	Most of the time.
LINDSAY	They can meddle a bit.
FISCHER	"A bit"?
LINDSAY	A lot.
FISCHER	At least they're happy we're moving into a white neighborhood.
LINDSAY	(*Making air quotes.*) They're "traditionalists."
SHANNY	Well, it's not an *entirely* white neighborhood.
MARTYN	The Helms across the street –

Shanny	They're a black family.
Martyn	Not that you'd notice.
Shanny	They fit right in.
Martyn	And that new couple at the end of the block.
Shanny	Right.
Martyn	(*Hasn't quite figured out their race.*) They're *something.*
Shanny	They fixed that house right up.
Martyn	Maybe Arab or Indian.
Shanny	Indian from India Indian.
Martyn	(*Making tomahawk gesture at* Fischer.) Not the tomahawk kind.
Shanny	(*To* Martyn.) What's that thing on the forehead?
Martyn	Eyebrow?
Shanny	(*Remembering.*) Bindi dot!
Martyn	Yes, right!
Shanny	The wife has no Bindi dot, so it's hard to tell.
Martyn	We'll probably never meet them now.
Fischer	Isn't that something you're supposed to disclose during the house sale?
Shanny	What?
Fischer	Who the neighbors are.
Martyn	Oh, they're all fine neighbors, no worries.

LINDSAY	None.
FISCHER	Would have been good to know –
LINDSAY	(*To* FISCHER.) It's okay.
FISCHER	Nothing against them. It's just the re-sale price –
LINDSAY	(*To* MARTYN *and* SHANNY.) It's fine.
FISCHER	Just seems like something you mention.
LINDSAY	Dear –
FISCHER	As a courtesy.
MARTYN	(*Good-naturedly.*) You're sounding a little biased there, Fischer.
FISCHER	I just worry about other people's biases when it's time to sell the place.
MARTYN	The Helms are no one to worry about.
LINDSAY	Of course.
MARTYN	They're like the black people in television commercials.
LINDSAY	We look forward to meeting them.
	(*The phone rings.* SHANNY *answers it.*)
SHANNY	Hello? (*Pause.*) Hi, dear. (*To* FISCHER *and* LINDSAY, *a bit pointedly.*) It's *Sarah.* (*Into phone.*) Yes, it's sold. You'll have to come back and help me box up what you want to keep. (*A pause, then she indicates the teddy bear.*) But I like your bear. It reminds me of you when you're away. (*Pause.*) It's not embarrassing, dear. (*Pause.*) Which campus protest? (*Pause.*) Yes, I'm sure haddock *do* have rights. (*Pause.*) Of course, of course,

get back to painting your placard. Keep your shirt on this time, dear.

(SHANNY *hangs up phone.*)

SHANNY   (*Exasperated.*) College!

MARTYN   Thinks she's going to save the world.

SHANNY   Start reading a few books and now they know everything.

MARTYN   *Everything.*

SHANNY   Our son used to love sports.

MARTYN   But now it's all books and ideas.

LINDSAY   What's he studying at college?

SHANNY   Philosophy.

MARTYN   For some reason he likes it.

SHANNY   (*Sarcastic.*) He's going to get a job in a big philosophy firm.

FISCHER   He's not gay too, is he?

MARTYN   Nope.

FISCHER   Because if this house turns people gay –

LINDSAY   Fischer –

FISCHER   I'm joking. Where it comes from is a mystery. Science is working on it.

(*An awkward pause, then* FISCHER *speaks.*)

FISCHER   May I go measure something?

MARTYN   Sure, fine.

(FISCHER *gets up, pulls a tape measure from his pocket and leaves the room.*)

LINDSAY   I'm sorry – Fischer's just anxious about the move.

MARTYN   No worries.

LINDSAY   Especially since he likes the place so much. And his work has been extra stressful lately.

MARTYN   I'm sure.

LINDSAY   (*To* SHANNY.) Do you have a job someplace?

SHANNY   Heck no.

MARTYN   She raised the kids.

LINDSAY   That's a noble sacrifice.

SHANNY   How so?

LINDSAY   Staying home is a totally valid option –

MARTYN   I told her she could work if she wanted to.

SHANNY   That was big of you, dear.

MARTYN   But either way was fine. Even if we needed the money.

SHANNY   He's a *dentist*. Dentists even retire early.

MARTYN   Nobody wants an old dentist.

SHANNY   They get sick of their patients –

MARTYN   No one wants an old dentist with shaking hands.

SHANNY   Sick of the patients with the bad breath.

MARTYN   That's a medical condition –

SHANNY	He's got nicknames for some of those. "Dead Mouse Debbie." "Professor Baby Diaper."
LINDSAY	I think Dead Mouse Debbie is the one from my office!
MARTYN	(*To* SHANNY, *irritated.*) Dang it, dear, you gave it away –
LINDSAY	"Dead Mouse" is generous of you.
MARTYN	(*Irritated.*) Shanny –
LINDSAY	I'd say more like "Amazon Latrine." "Amazon Latrine After Monkey Lasagne"!
	(FISCHER *re-enters, holding the tape measure.*)
FISCHER	(*To* LINDSAY.) Yep, it's too small now.
LINDSAY	Ah – that's what I was afraid of.
SHANNY	What is?
FISCHER	The breakfast nook.
LINDSAY	We bought a big beautiful antique breakfast table.
FISCHER	And sideboard. Plus this nice shelving from our current place. (*To* LINDSAY.) I'll call some contractors tomorrow.
LINDSAY	(*Now wanting to stop the line of conversation.*) Fischer –
FISCHER	To get some estimates.
LINDSAY	(*Wanting him to stop.*) Honey –
MARTYN	Estimates for what?
FISCHER	Expanding the kitchen.

> (*There's a brief, uncertain pause all around.*
> *Then* MARTYN *speaks.*)

MARTYN   Expand the kitchen?

FISCHER   Into the backyard.

SHANNY   Oh.

FISCHER   It's a little tight as is, with all this new stuff.

MARTYN   Into the backyard?

LINDSAY   Not a lot.

FISCHER   (*Trying to reassure.*) Same style as the rest of the house.

LINDSAY   Right.

FISCHER   About fifteen feet, as long as we're building.

MARTYN   You're going to change the house?

FISCHER   Extend off the rear.

SHANNY   But that's where my garden is.

LINDSAY   Oh, the garden is beautiful.

SHANNY   My azaleas and morning glories –

LINDSAY   It looks like we need the room.

MARTYN   (*Good-naturedly.*) The kitchen's worked pretty well for us like it is –

LINDSAY   Oh, I'm sure.

MARTYN   Eat breakfast in there every morning.

LINDSAY   I'm sure it's been great for you.

FISCHER   We have all this new stuff –

MARTYN   It's a pretty good kitchen.

LINDSAY   It's just not going to fit.

                   (*Pause.*)

LINDSAY   I'm sorry, we didn't know for sure till just now.

MARTYN   (*Upbeat.*) Maybe you could use your table in
                   the dining room.

SHANNY   Plenty of room in there for it.

LINDSAY   The table is for a kitchen.

FISCHER   The kitchen is a shade small anyway.

MARTYN   You admired it during the house tours.

LINDSAY   It's lovely, it is.

FISCHER   The extension will have the same design.

LINDSAY   And a nice bay window.

SHANNY   But it would be on my garden.

LINDSAY   I'm so sorry about that.

MARTYN   Is that necessary?

LINDSAY   I'm afraid so.

FISCHER   That's just where the kitchen is.

LINDSAY   And we're not really gardeners anyway.

FISCHER   No time –

LINDSAY   It'd wither away with us.

(*Pause.*)

SHANNY   (*Upbeat.*) Well, look – once you move in, you'll
                see. You'll like the kitchen!

MARTYN   You will!

SHANNY   Once you're in here, you'll see how well that
                kitchen works.

MARTYN   You bet.

SHANNY   The set-up is pretty perfect, with the stove and
                the counter –

MARTYN   And the nook where it is.

SHANNY   We'll have you over for dinner before you move
                in – see how great it is at meal time.

MARTYN   With some nice wine and one of Shanny's pork
                loins.

LINDSAY   It's the size –

SHANNY   (*To* MARTYN.) Haven't had anyone for dinner in
                ages.

MARTYN   Too long.

SHANNY   Since the Vernons.

MARTYN   Tom Vernon loved Shanny's loins.

SHANNY   (*Indicating intestines.*) Before his blockage.

MARTYN   What night works best?

LINDSAY   Thank you, but we need an extension –

MARTYN   But why put up with all that construction mess?

SHANNY   And those builders in your house.

MARTYN   You don't want strangers in your house when
                you're at work all day.

SHANNY   They start nosing around.

MARTYN   Looking in your drawers.

SHANNY   Try out your shampoos.

LINDSAY   (*More emphatically.*) Really, we need to build it.

                (*A pause as* MARTYN *and* SHANNY *take in* LINDSAY'*s
                comment.*)

MARTYN   It would destroy her garden.

LINDSAY   (*Being nice.*) I know.

MARTYN   She's worked on that garden for years.

LINDSAY   You can tell.

SHANNY   I built it up like that. With the flowers and the
                levels –

MARTYN   (*Re.* SHANNY.) Out there on her knees.

SHANNY   It's got tricky sunlight.

MARTYN   She *loves* that garden.

SHANNY   You can sit in the nook at breakfast and look at
                it while you eat your cantaloupe.

MARTYN   Lawyers eat cantaloupe, right?

LINDSAY   Sometimes.

                (*Pause.*)

MARTYN   (*To* FISCHER, *man-to-man.*) Look, how about if we
                lower the price a little.

SHANNY	(*To* MARTYN.) That's probably what they want.
FISCHER	The sale price?
MARTYN	Drop it down a little, then keep the kitchen like it is.
SHANNY	Yes, we could do that.
MARTYN	Would be worth it to us.
LINDSAY	But you've already given us such a good price –
MARTYN	This way we know the house would stay the same. Without any confusion this time.
LINDSAY	That's a kind offer –
MARTYN	We'll get by without the extra money.
LINDSAY	A kind offer, but it doesn't line up with what we need here.
MARTYN	We can order some new paperwork –
FISCHER	Thank you for offering, but no.
	(*Pause.*)
MARTYN	Really?
LINDSAY	I'm afraid so.
	(*Pause.*)
MARTYN	I guess we hadn't thought there'd be any changes once we sold it.
SHANNY	No.
MARTYN	So you see why we're a little confused all of a sudden. Selling it is a big thing for us.

LINDSAY	Oh, naturally.
MARTYN	So we just have certain expectations. And you seemed so enthusiastic about it the way it is.
LINDSAY	We've been very excited.
MARTYN	Right – so of course we assume, you know, that means excited about what the house is now.
FISCHER	We're very happy to have bought it.
MARTYN	Good, good. It's just sort of a different thing you want to do there.
LINDSAY	It'll still be a great house.
FISCHER	With just a bigger kitchen.
MARTYN	But it's more complicated than that.
SHANNY	We're selling it like it is –
MARTYN	So the new people can have what we had.
SHANNY	But if you have plans to change it, change the house, we may have to think about this some more then.
MARTYN	Yes –
SHANNY	Sit down and think if this is what we really want to do now –
MARTYN	That would be a good idea –
SHANNY	If this is the sale we want to make.
LINDSAY	I'm afraid the house is sold –
SHANNY	Because it's such a big decision –
MARTYN	To see if it's still right for us now.

SHANNY	Because it's our home.
MARTYN	It's why we were selling it ourselves –
SHANNY	To make sure the next owners were the right people for it.
MARTYN	If you lived here, you'd understand.
FISCHER	(*Emphatically.*) We *will* live here.
SHANNY	We can't just abandon it.
LINDSAY	You're not abandoning it.
SHANNY	We could never move otherwise.
MARTYN	It'd never be the same place with a change like that.
SHANNY	Even if we never saw, we'd know.
MARTYN	Could never even drive past.
	(*Pause.*)
SHANNY	Yes, I'm sorry, but Martyn and I have to talk about this now. This was maybe all a little quick and premature. Thank you for coming today. I'm sorry this is sort of sudden like this. But it's new news. We'll have to talk about it and get back to you to see if we still want to go through with it.
MARTYN	Yes – yes, that's a good idea.
FISCHER	You already decided.
LINDSAY	You signed the papers.
SHANNY	No –
FISCHER	You did!

LINDSAY   It's done.

MARTYN   We need to re-think.

FISCHER   You can't.

MARTYN   Since this has come up now.

SHANNY   (*To* LINDSAY *and* FISCHER.) If you'd said something.

FISCHER   When you sell a house, you sell a house.

MARTYN   But this one's different.

LINDSAY   No one moves into a house and keeps it exactly the same.

FISCHER   *Nobody.*

MARTYN   But this is the house you saw.

LINDSAY   I know –

MARTYN   You saw *this* house.

SHANNY   We didn't give them permission to change anything.

MARTYN   No.

SHANNY   When did we okay that?

FISCHER   There's no law against home improvement.

SHANNY   "Improvement"?

FISCHER   Once you own a place.

LINDSAY   We're allowed to fix things to make it better –

SHANNY   Better?

LINDSAY   A little nicer.

SHANNY	How could it be *nicer?*
LINDSAY	Shanny –
SHANNY	No – I'm sorry. We may have to cancel.
FISCHER	You can't.
MARTYN	(*Convinced.*) Yes, she's right.
SHANNY	We'll take those papers back for now.
LINDSAY	The house is *ours.*
FISCHER	*Legally.*
SHANNY	No –
FISCHER	*Yes.*
SHANNY	Why like a house so much, then ruin it?
LINDSAY	Ruin it?
SHANNY	For a table.
LINDSAY	It's a beautiful antique –
SHANNY	A table isn't better because Amish people ate off it!
LINDSAY	The table is French –
SHANNY	Leave my kitchen alone!
LINDSAY	(*Trying to convince* SHANNY *and* MARTYN.) It'll be a good kitchen –
FISCHER	Pretty.
LINDSAY	With more counter space.
FISCHER	An ice maker.

LINDSAY	A spice shelf.
FISCHER	Wine rack.
LINDSAY	Cute porcelain teapots.
FISCHER	And we don't drink tea.
SHANNY	Lawyers can't even cook!
LINDSAY	(*Offended.*) Oh, I can cook. I got recipes –
SHANNY	So?
LINDSAY	Timers!
SHANNY	(*Sarcastically.*) Whoa!
LINDSAY	And four meat thermometers!
SHANNY	No! It's *my* kitchen! Mine! So don't you –
MARTYN	(*Abruptly, distressed, and loudly.*) Murphy!!!
SHANNY	(*Distressed and loudly.*) Murphy!
MARTYN	(*Distressed and loudly.*) Murphy!
SHAN. / MART.	(*Distressed and loudly.*) Murphy!!!
LINDSAY	Who?
MARTYN	(*Pointing at* LINDSAY.) Murphy!
SHANNY	He's buried in the garden!
FISCHER	You killed someone?!
MARTYN	Our dog!
SHANNY	In the garden –
SHAN. / MART.	(*Together.*) Murphy!

MARTYN   Oh, no!

SHANNY   We loved him.

MARTYN   Oh, man, Murphy!

SHANNY   Big Irish Setter –

MARTYN   A sweetheart.

SHANNY   He'd smile, I swear –

MARTYN   The kids *loved* him.

SHANNY   He loved *them*.

MARTYN   So loyal –

SHANNY   So kind!

MARTYN   A little bit farty.

SHANNY   A *lot* farty.

MARTYN   The bad ones you couldn't get out of your
                  clothes!

SHAN. / MART.   (*Together.*) Murphy!

SHANNY   (*To* FISCHER *and* LINDSAY.) Now you want to dig
                  him up!

MARTYN   To build on the garden!

SHANNY   His bones!

MARTYN   When you build the new *wing* –

FISCHER   It needs a foundation!

SHAN. / MART.   Murphy!

SHANNY   So friendly.

MARTYN	Lift his paw and shake without asking.
SHANNY	When you walked in the room!
MARTYN	Like a good bartender.
FISCHER	We'll give you his bones back.
SHANNY	What?!
FISCHER	When we dig him up –
LINDSAY	You can re-bury him somewhere else –
FISCHER	Or reassemble them.
SHAN. / MART.	(*Together.*) *Reassemble them?!*
LINDSAY	Since you miss him so much –
FISCHER	(*Holding his hand out.*) In a shaking pose.

(SHANNY *jumps up and grabs and rips up* SHANNY *and* MARTYN'S *copy of the sale documents.*)

SHANNY	No! No, they can't have it! It's canceled! Right now!

(SHANNY *moves toward* FISCHER *and* LINDSAY'S *copy.*)

SHANNY	Give me those papers!
LINDSAY	No!
SHANNY	*Give them to me!*

(SHANNY *has gotten ahold of the contract copy, but* FISCHER *and* LINDSAY *try to grab it from her hands. Everyone has ahold of it now, a big group struggle.*)

FISCHER	What are you doing?!

SHANNY   You're not getting it –

MARTYN   Honey!

SHANNY   None of it –

FISCHER   Let go!

SHANNY   The house –

LINDSAY   It's . . . *ours!*

              (LINDSAY *manages to yank the contract file away
              from* SHANNY, *but gives* FISCHER *a big cut on his
              hand.*)

FISCHER   (*Recoiling.*) Damn it!

LINDSAY   What the hell?

FISCHER   Sliced me!

MARTYN   Shanny!

LINDSAY   (*To* SHANNY.) What are you doing?

FISCHER   (*Showing his bleeding hand.*) My hand –

LINDSAY   (*To* FISCHER.) You're bleeding –

SHANNY   It's *our* house!

LINDSAY   He's bleeding!

MARTYN   I'll get him something –

SHANNY   Don't!

FISCHER   (*Re. cut.*) Damn, that hurts.

MARTYN   I'll get the first-aid kit –

SHANNY   (*Trying to stop him.*) Martyn!

(MARTYN *exits to get a first-aid kit.*)

FISCHER   (*Re. his painful hand.*) Jesus –

LINDSAY   (*To* SHANNY.) You can't just do things like that.

SHANNY   Tell that to my garden.

LINDSAY   (*To* SHANNY.) Just calm down –

SHANNY   You should see how beautiful it's been this year.

LINDSAY   If it were in a different place –

SHANNY   You'd build something there too!

LINDSAY   No –

SHANNY   A gazpacho.

LINDSAY   What?

SHANNY   Build a big wooden gazpacho on it!

LINDSAY   A gazebo?

SHANNY   Sure, gazebo!

                 (MARTYN *re-enters with first-aid kit, a bottle of antiseptic alcohol, and a towel. He gives the towel to* FISCHER.)

MARTYN   Here –

LINDSAY   (*To* SHANNY.) You can't rip up signed contracts. They'd still be binding.

SHANNY   There's nothing in them about a new breakfast room!

FISCHER   You sold it. It's gone!

MARTYN   Maybe you say something about it first.

(MARTYN *aggressively splashes antiseptic alcohol onto* FISCHER'S *hand,* FISCHER *yelping in pain.*)

LINDSAY   (*Re. cut.*) This is no way to act.

SHANNY   If we knew –

MARTYN   We would have kept it.

SHANNY   Or picked someone else.

MARTYN   Somebody better!

SHANNY   (*To* MARTYN.) That other couple.

MARTYN   Who made the higher offer.

SHANNY   Kind people.

MARTYN   Honest.

SHANNY   And so good-looking.

MARTYN   Like a Hollywood couple.

SHANNY   They were the right choice.

MARTYN   (*Re.* FISCHER *and* LINDSAY.) Not them!

FISCHER   (*Patience gone.*) Oh, so sorry we're not from Hollywood. So sorry we've never been in rehab. So sorry we've never starred in some blockbuster about aliens coming down and destroying cities in a plot to . . . to . . . get in the newspaper! Now I gotta use the bathroom!

              (FISCHER *begins to exit.*)

SHANNY   Oh, no you're not!

FISCHER   I'm using the bathroom in *my new house.*

SHANNY   (*To* MARTYN.) Stop him!

FISCHER	Back in a bit!
SHANNY	It better be number one!
MARTYN	Damn right!
FISCHER	(*Stopping his exit, taunting.*) Well, I don't know. It *could* be number one. But it might be number two.
MARTYN	Damn well better not be!
FISCHER	It might be a number-one-and-two combo.
SHANNY	Jesus –
FISCHER	It might be a one-and-two *special edition!*
	(FISCHER *exits.*)
SHANNY	(*To* MARTYN.) Go get him outta there.
LINDSAY	We can use the bathroom –
SHANNY	Before he puts his hairy butt on my toilet seat.
LINDSAY	It's *our* toilet seat!
SHANNY	(*To* MARTYN.) You didn't stop him.
MARTYN	I tried –
SHANNY	Now he's in there. Using *our* toilet paper. Breathing our potpourri –
MARTYN	(*Defensively.*) I know –
SHANNY	While you just *stand around.* Stand around like a *dentist!*
LINDSAY	I'm sorry about McCarthy.
SHAN. / MART.	(*Correcting.*) *Murphy!*

LINDSAY	I'm sorry about the kitchen. But it's ours and we can do what we want.
MARTYN	It wasn't the deal.
LINDSAY	You're just having seller's regret. You sell and subconscious emotions all start coming out.
MARTYN	That's claptrap!
LINDSAY	Read the Sunday magazine! Feelings of loss and doubt and stupidity –
MARTYN	We are not stupid!
SHANNY	Or fools!
MARTYN	Or chumps!
SHANNY	Or idiots.
MARTYN	Or blockheads!
	(*Brief pause.*)
SHANNY	(*In despair.*) Yes we are!
	(FISCHER *re-enters.*)
FISCHER	(*Indicating his bandaged hand.*) I couldn't wash my hands.
LINDSAY	(*Alarmed*) Fischer –
FISCHER	It's their fault.
LINDSAY	Go try.
FISCHER	(*Indicating bandage.*) I can't.
LINDSAY	Go *wash* them!
FISCHER	They're fine.

LINDSAY   Not again.

FISCHER   Please –

LINDSAY   How many times, Fischer?

FISCHER   Don't start.

LINDSAY   Clean them!

FISCHER   I won't touch you.

LINDSAY   (*Retreating from* FISCHER.) Now!

FISCHER   I won't –

LINDSAY   (*Pointing to* FISCHER'*s hands.*) Microbes!

FISCHER   Lindsay –

LINDSAY   *Tiny microbes!!*

SHANNY   Oh, Jesus – what have we done? Did we really
               sell it? And to these two?

FISCHER   Damn right you did!

SHANNY   After all we've put into it. We should have
               guessed this would happen.

MARTYN   We didn't know –

SHANNY   Suspected the worst.

MARTYN   They seemed nice.

SHANNY   The neighbors – what have we done to them all
               by selling?!

MARTYN   They trusted us.

SHANNY   Always.

MARTYN	After how long we lived here –
SHANNY	All we did for them.
MARTYN	Loaned tools.
MARTYN	Baby-sat sick kids.
SHANNY	All night cleaning up the Jello vomit.
MARTYN	(*Pointing at* FISCHER *and* LINDSAY.) But we sold to *them!*
SHANNY	To deceivers.
MARTYN	They'll never forgive us!
SHANNY	There'll be no more invitations.
MARTYN	No graduation parties.
SHANNY	No barbecues.
MARTYN	I *love* Bill's barbecues!
SHANNY	Oh, dear –
MARTYN	Bill's burgers –
SHANNY	Each summer!
MARTYN	(*To* FISCHER *and* LINDSAY, *angrily.*) He makes them with *soy sauce!*
FISCHER	I'll eat one for you.
MARTYN	They're eating our burgers! (*To* FISCHER *and* LINDSAY.) No! It's *our* neighborhood. *We* go to Bill's. *We* eat the burgers. *I* win the lawn bowling!
SHANNY	You should let a kid win sometime –

MARTYN   Then they never get better!

SHANNY   To encourage them –

MARTYN   Encouragement is condescending!

FISCHER   I'm letting a kid win at lawn bowling!

MARTYN   They won't let you in.

FISCHER   We'll bring a piñata.

MARTYN   Won't work!

FISCHER   No one in the history of parties has been
                turned away when they brought a piñata! I can
                already smell the grill smoke drifting down the
                block. The charcoal and sizzling meat. It's why
                we'll love this suburb, babe. Cookouts! Trees!
                Brick patios! The chirping robins and buzzing
                cicadas –

MARTYN   No! No, those are *our cicadas!*

LINDSAY   It's sold!

SHANNY   We made it what it is.

FISCHER   You signed the contract!

LINDSAY   You've got a new home –

FISCHER   Your condo.

SHANNY   I can't believe this is happening.

MARTYN   I know –

SHANNY   It seemed so simple.

MARTYN   It was.

SHANNY   Find the right people.

MARTYN   Who'd respect it.

SHANNY   Love it.

MARTYN   Take care of it.

SHANNY   For years and years.

MARTYN   *This* house.

SHANNY   My kitchen.

MARTYN   The garden.

SHANNY   They liked it.

MARTYN   Every room.

SHANNY   And now they act –

MARTYN   I know!

SHANNY   Like . . . like . . . like . . . *bastards.*

            (*Abrupt pause.*)

FISCHER   (*Taken aback, then speaks.*) Excuse me?

            (SHANNY *refuses to reply.*)

FISCHER   We're what?

            (SHANNY *still refuses to answer.* FISCHER *waits, then speaks.*)

FISCHER   That's it – get out.

SHANNY   No!

MARTYN   We've got a lease.

FISCHER   No, you're outta here.

MARTYN   *Ten* weeks!

FISCHER   Go!

MARTYN   It's ours at least till then!

FISCHER   Screw that!

LINDSAY   (*To* FISCHER.) We agreed –

FISCHER   Just screw it! Start packing – *now!*

                (FISCHER *starts pacing around the room in
                agitation.*)

LINDSAY   (*To* FISCHER.) Calm down –

FISCHER   Try to do them a goddamn favor, try to be nice –

SHANNY   Not budging!

FISCHER   Then start calling us names. Pack! All of it!
                (*Pointing.*) The sofas, the paintings, the pictures –

SHANNY   Never!

FISCHER   The TV, the curtains, the lamp –

                (FISCHER *grabs the lamp.*)

FISCHER   The cushions, the coasters –

LINDSAY   Calm down –

FISCHER   Take it!

                (FISCHER *thrusts the lamp he's holding at* SHANNY
                *while she's moving toward him. It accidentally
                hits her jaw.*)

SHANNY   *Oww!*

MARTYN   Honey!

SHANNY	*Oww! Oww!*
MARTYN	(*To* FISCHER.) What the –
LINDSAY	Fischer!
	(SHANNY's *mouth is bleeding.*)
SHANNY	My mouth –
MARTYN	Dear!
SHANNY	My tooth!
MARTYN	Jesus –
SHANNY	It's loose.
MARTYN	Dammit, let me see –
LINDSAY	Christ, Fischer!
FISCHER	They gotta move –
LINDSAY	They will!
MARTYN	(*To* SHANNY *re. mouth.*) Open –
FISCHER	They gotta go.
MARTYN	(*To* SHANNY *re. tooth.*) Which one?
SHANNY	(*To* MARTYN.) There –
MARTYN	That one?
SHANNY	My cuspid!
MARTYN	(*Correcting.*) Bicuspid.
LINDSAY	(*To* MARTYN *and* SHANNY.) He didn't mean it.
	(MARTYN *pokes at* SHANNY's *tooth.*)

MARTYN   This one?!

LINDSAY   (*To* FISCHER.) Fischer!

MARTYN   The periodontal membrane is torn. (*To* FISCHER
              and LINDSAY.) A second-degree periodontal
              rupture with fissure of the left mandibular first
              bicuspid, *number twenty-one!*

LINDSAY   Are you sure?

MARTYN   (*To* FISCHER.) This is going to cost you!

LINDSAY   I don't believe you.

MARTYN   (*Pointing to* SHANNY'S *mouth.*) Look!

LINDSAY   Where?

MARTYN   (*Putting finger in* SHANNY'S *mouth.*) There, for
              Christsake!

LINDSAY   Which one?!

MARTYN   *This* one!

              (*In frustration,* MARTYN *yanks out the loose
              tooth.*)

SHANNY   (*Recoiling in pain.*) Eehyeh!

              (FISCHER *and* LINDSAY *recoil from where they
              stand.*)

MARTYN   (*Holding up the tooth to* FISCHER *and* LINDSAY.)
              This one, goddamnit! First left mandibular!
              What the hell else does it look like?! (*Points at*
              FISCHER.) *He* did this!

LINDSAY   Put the cuspid down –

MARTYN   *Bi*-cuspid!

FISCHER	(*Pointing at the tooth with "ick" face.*) Is that a nerve?
MARTYN	Damn right!
	(FISCHER *reacts badly to this.*)
SHANNY	Why did you –
MARTYN	(*To* SHANNY.) It had to come out –
SHANNY	You ripped it –
MARTYN	Too damaged –
SHANNY	My mouth –
MARTYN	(*To* FISCHER *and* LINDSAY.) She'll need an implant. You're paying for it!
FISCHER	The hell I am.
MARTYN	Two thousand bucks!
LINDSAY	We'll pay it.
FISCHER	Two thousand?!
LINDSAY	It's cheaper than getting sued –
FISCHER	Old, weak teeth. God know what she's been chewing on all these years –
LINDSAY	It doesn't matter –
FISCHER	Think of what they ate back then!
LINDSAY	We have to.
FISCHER	It's too much!
LINDSAY	(*To* FISCHER.) Calm down! Everybody just calm down. *Please!* (*To* FISCHER.) Get her some water.

FISCHER   Me?

LINDSAY   Do it!

                 (FISCHER *exits to get some water.* LINDSAY *is
                 flustered. There's an awkward long moment as
                 things calm down. Then* LINDSAY, *trying to be
                 nice, speaks.*)

LINDSAY   How . . . How is it feeling?

                 (SHANNY *tongues where her tooth used to be.
                 Then speaks.*)

SHANNY   I got a hole in my gum as big as a vagina.

                 (FISCHER *re-enters with a glass of water.*)

LINDSAY   We're very sorry about your tooth.

FISCHER   (*Conceding.*) Okay.

LINDSAY   And the shouting.

FISCHER   Sorry about that.

LINDSAY   That should never have happened. We're very,
                 very sorry. Really. And we're sorry about any
                 misunderstanding with the kitchen. If we had
                 different expectations there. Of course that kind
                 of change could cause concern. I'm truly sorry
                 about any distress it's causing. And again, about
                 the tooth.

                 (*Pause.*)

MARTYN   No. No, apology not accepted. The only
                 apology now is giving us the house back.

LINDSAY   That can't happen.

MARTYN   You can – right now! We'll all agree to it –

LINDSAY   No.

MARTYN   This minute –

FISCHER   Nope –

MARTYN   You don't deserve it! (*To* SHANNY.) Not them.
               (*To* FISCHER *and* LINDSAY.) Destroy our kitchen.
               Dig up our dog. Insult our daughter, a possible
               lesbian. No, this place deserves someone
               better. Respectful people. Decent, good people.
               Not Mr and Mrs Asshole from Asshole Street,
               Asshole Town! (*Brief pause, then thinking of
               another.*) State of Asshole!

FISCHER   (*Calmly to* LINDSAY.) Give me your purse.

               (LINDSAY *hands* FISCHER *her purse.* FISCHER *reaches
               in and pulls out a huge handful of paint
               swatches.*)

FISCHER   Amazing how many colors they have these
               days. You'd think they'd have figured them all
               out a long time ago, but they keep coming up
               with new ones.

               (FISCHER *starts flipping the swatches into the room
               as he names the color of each, becoming more
               aggressive as he goes.*)

FISCHER   Red and blue, sure, but how about Wild
               Currant? Some Ember Glow and Spiced Cedar?
               Fireweed, Obstinate Orange, Tiger Eye, and
               Aristocratic Peach? Turkish Coffee, Porpoise,
               Alpaca, Cut the Mustard, Social Butterfly, High
               Tea, Hunt Club, and Kismet!

SHANNY   Why do you have all these?

FISCHER   (*Snapping, and throwing all the remaining
               swatches into the air.*) 'Cause it's all changing!

MARTYN   What?

FISCHER   All the colors, all the walls! Not just the
                kitchen. And the tiles, the carpets, the bushes,
                the goddamn flagpole!

SHANNY   No!

LINDSAY   You sold it –

FISCHER   Tearing out the dining room wall. The basketball
                hoop, the weather rooster on the roof!

MARTYN   It's a weather *squirrel!*

FISCHER   It's gone! The fridge, the Home Sweet Home
                welcome mat –

SHANNY   *You can't!*

FISCHER   Where's that in the contract?

SHANNY   But –

FISCHER   Nowhere!

MARTYN   I nearly killed myself putting up that weather
                squirrel!

LINDSAY   It's gone! And the oven and shutters and drawer
                handles.

FISCHER   New windows!

LINDSAY   Light fixtures!

FISCHER   Bookcases!

LINDSAY   Finish the basement –

FISCHER   New showerheads –

LINDSAY   Central air, new front door –

FISCHER	A patio off the kitchen extension.
LINDSAY	Cut down that pine tree.
FISCHER	To get some light in here!
LINDSAY	Some sun!
FISCHER	(*Pointing offstage.*) And the hallway!
SHANNY	What about it?
FISCHER	You know what about it.
LINDSAY	That thing!
SHANNY	What thing?
FISCHER	It's outta here!
LINDSAY	How could you put it there?
SHANNY	What?!
LINDSAY	I'll show you!
	(LINDSAY *exits quickly.*)
FISCHER	You actually keep it there –
SHANNY	(*To* MARTYN.) Make them stop –
FISCHER	In plain sight!
SHANNY	They're impossible!
FISCHER	*We* are?
SHANNY	Both of you.
FISCHER	This house is going to look right!
MARTYN	Never!

FISCHER   Once the *tenants* are gone.

                   (LINDSAY *re-enters holding a large bowling
                   trophy, but at the top, instead of a man, there's
                   a very large tooth bowling a ball. She holds it
                   up high.*)

LINDSAY   *This* thing!

MARTYN   My trophy!

FISCHER   Right!

MARTYN   So dentists like to bowl –

LINDSAY   It's a bowling *tooth!*

MARTYN   (*Specifying.*) A bowling *molar!*

LINDSAY   (*In disbelief.*) Look at it!

MARTYN   We have a dentists' league!

FISCHER   Thank god it's not a league for gynecologists.

LINDSAY   It's hideous!

MARTYN   But we won!

FISCHER   (*Taking in the house.*) The potential is all here.

LINDSAY   To be completely what we imagined –

FISCHER   An amazing place.

LINDSAY   On the perfect block.

FISCHER   In the perfect location.

LINDSAY   In the best school district.

FISCHER   The home of homes –

LIND. / FISCH.	*Our dream house!*
SHANNY	Full of sewage back-up!
	(*Startled pause.*)
LINDSAY	What?
MARTYN	It sometimes flows the wrong direction –
SHANNY	From the whole block –
MARTYN	A bad way to get to know your neighbors.
FISCHER	Now wait a minute –
SHANNY	And fix the roof while you're up there tearing down that weather squirrel!
LINDSAY	What about it?
MARTYN	And rip out that furnace!
LINDSAY	You said it was new!
MARTYN	It is.
SHANNY	New and *defective.*
MARTYN	(*Pointing at* FISCHER *and* LINDSAY.) Sweaters!
FISCHER	That's crap!
MARTYN	(*To* SHANNY.) I hope they like asbestos.
FISCHER	Asbestos?!
MARTYN	They *loved* it back then!
SHANNY	Your inspector missed a whole area!
LINDSAY	That's ridiculous.

FISCHER   Sewage!

MARTYN   Bad city engineering.

LINDSAY   So you lied to us –

SHANNY   You didn't ask the right questions.

FISCHER   Hid things, eh?!

LINDSAY   A lying dentist! A lying Down's Syndrome
               mother –

SHANNY   She's fine!

LINDSAY   (*Indicating photo.*) No, she isn't! She looks
               completely retarded!

MARTYN   (*Trying to defend.*) She looks like her mother!

SHANNY   She's not retarded, she's an art major!

LINDSAY   That proves it!

FISCHER   You didn't tell us about *any* of those things.

SHANNY   (*Sarcastically.*) Oops!

FISCHER   Lying about a house sale – is that part of
               Episcopalianism?

SHANNY   Of course not –

FISCHER   The priest teaching how to cheat on real-estate
               deals?

MARTYN   Stay out of that church!

SHANNY   It's a church for *good people.*

MARTYN   People with souls.

LINDSAY   I have a soul!

SHANNY   No one with a soul would change this house.

FISCHER   Our souls are fine!

MARTYN   They seem pretty rusty to me –

SHANNY   Decrepit!

MARTYN   Like some clunky old car.

FISCHER   Ours are like new!

SHANNY   Hardly!

FISCHER   Like right from the showroom!

MARTYN   Ours are bigger and better!

SHANNY   Like a Cadillac.

MARTYN   A Rolls Royce!

FISCHER   Ours are a limo.

MARTYN   Ours are a limo with a wet bar!

FISCHER   Ours are a limo with a wet bar and strippers!

LINDSAY   (*To* FISCHER.) What?!

FISCHER   (*To* LINDSAY.) You know what I mean! (*To* MARTYN
            and SHANNY.) So don't you go comparing souls!

LINDSAY   (*To* FISCHER.) Strippers?!

FISCHER   Lindsay –

LINDSAY   Everything isn't *strippers*, Fischer!

FISCHER   You can't still be mad about that –

LINDSAY   No?!

FISCHER	It was a bachelor party –
LINDSAY	(*Sarcastically.*) Great –
FISCHER	No one goes to a bachelor *brunch!* It's a *tradition.*
LINDSAY	Stop –
FISCHER	Like a baby shower –
LINDSAY	*Baby shower?*
FISCHER	It is!
LINDSAY	A baby shower has *cute* things! Little booties. Not some girl named Candy rubbing her crotch –
FISCHER	Her name was *Raven!*
SHANNY	This house is going to be full of strippers –
FISCHER	No it isn't –
SHANNY	(*To* LINDSAY.) Good luck, sweetie – I know where this ends up.
LINDSAY	(*To* SHANNY.) You stay out of this!
SHANNY	(*To* MARTYN.) They always fall for the bad boys.
LINDSAY	(*Pointing at* FISCHER.) He's a wimp!
SHANNY	Then next they're sipping wine at the divorced-ladies' bar.
FISCHER	We're not divorcing!
MARTYN	(*To* FISCHER *and* LINDSAY.) It's hell on kids, divorce.
SHANNY	Dave and Peggy's kid –
MARTYN	Seemed fine at first –

SHANNY	Then *bingo!*
MARTYN	They started finding cat parts in the backyard.
LINDSAY	We're not divorcing! Our kids will not have divorced parents!
FISCHER	Never!
LINDSAY	Their parents will love them –
FISCHER	And sacrifice for them –
LINDSAY	*Here*, in *this* house, by *two* parents whose marriage is *always intact*.
FISCHER	(*To* MARTYN *and* SHANNY.) No matter how many strippers!
LINDSAY	In this neighborhood, where it's *other kids* screwed up from divorce. Other kids with the scratching problem. Other kids sent to under-researched summer camps –
FISCHER	Everyone's going to like our kids!
LINDSAY	*Damn* right.
FISCHER	(*Indicating the house.*) This is where the other kids will all hang out –
LINDSAY	Here!
FISCHER	Video games –
LINDSAY	Air hockey –
FISCHER	Fridges full of soda –
LINDSAY	(*At* MARTYN *and* SHANNY.) And cheeses!
MARTYN	(*Sarcastically.*) Oh, I'm sure your kids will be really likeable.

| SHANNY | Win the Nobel Prize for Teenage Popularity. |

| FISCHER | Our kids will be great! |

| LINDSAY | Behave. |

| FISCHER | Obey their parents. |

| LINDSAY | And act nice – |

| SHANNY | Oh, it all sounds so easy! |

| MARTYN | (*Re.* FISCHER *and* LINDSAY.) Like they only know about kids from a brochure. |

| SHANNY | Your little baby – one day that head will be filled with sarcasm! |

| MARTYN | And reasons why the car is missing. |

| SHANNY | Just wait till you have your own. |

| LINDSAY | Oh, there's no waiting. I'm getting pregnant as soon as we move in! |

| FISCHER | (*Embarrassed.*) Dear – |

| LINDSAY | In *your* bedroom. |

| FISCHER | Lindsay – |

| LINDSAY | The *first* night. While it still has *your* carpeting. (*Points at* MARTYN.) Still smells like old-man after-shave. Then nine months later – (*Thrusting her hips at* MARTYN *and* SHANNY.) *boom!* – out pops Fischer Jr. or little Jessie. |

| FISCHER | (*To* LINDSAY.) I said not "Jessie" – |

| LINDSAY | I like it! |

| FISCHER | That was my gecko's name – |

LINDSAY   (*To* FISCHER.) But it's dead! (*To everyone.*) Then
                 you'll see what a good parent I am. *Everyone*
                 will see. I'll buy the softest baby clothes, the
                 newest crib. You'll see! They'll *all* see! All
                 those women at the firm with their attitude and
                 nannies. Desks loaded with pictures – kids with
                 cute missing teeth the mother *punched out*
                 right before to make the picture more adorable.
                 Well, I'll have *my* children now! They can look
                 at *my* pictures. *My* kids in soccer uniforms. At
                 the zoo. In Halloween costumes, dressed as
                 a cowboy or ballerina or some sort of British
                 person!

FISCHER   Just not "Jessie."

LINDSAY   Our child will not look like a lizard!

FISCHER   I know –

LINDSAY   No one in my family looks like a lizard –

FISCHER   (*Countering.*) Aunt Jane.

LINDSAY   That was from a *car accident!*

SHANNY   (*Despairing.*) *Their* kids running around –

MARTYN   I know.

SHANNY   Those should be our grandchildren playing
                 here –

FISCHER   (*Suddenly inspired.*) I'll build our kids a tree fort.

MARTYN   They'll break their necks!

LINDSAY   No they won't –

MARTYN   The town is full of paralyzed kids. Kids who
                 begged for a tree fort. Begged and begged so
                 they could play Old West or Jungle Bride, but

	then slip over the edge and snap their spinal cord.
SHANNY	Those parents should be arrested.
MARTYN	Yes!
SHANNY	Instead they want sympathy!
MARTYN	As the town fills up with crippled kids. You've never seen a sadder ice cream parlor!
FISCHER	We're having coordinated kids who don't plummet from things –
LINDSAY	They won't smoke pot, even though it makes you popular.
FISCHER	*Crazy* popular.
LINDSAY	They'll be popular for the *right* reasons.
FISCHER	All of them.
LINDSAY	A million friends.
FISCHER	Not some misfit who dies and no one cries about at graduation.
LINDSAY	If our kid dies, *everyone* is crying at graduation.
FISCHER	But they're *not* dying.
LINDSAY	No!
FISCHER	That's why we live in the suburbs –
LINDSAY	Dying in high school is for *city* kids.
FISCHER	We'll have good kids who never get arrested.
LINDSAY	No late-night calls from the station house for us!

MARTYN	The police in this town are useless!
SHANNY	(*To* MARTYN.) They never solved that burglary.
LINDSAY	Burglary?
MARTYN	Around the corner.
SHANNY	While everyone was sleeping!
MARTYN	Walked right in –
SHANNY	Stole the flat-screen.
MARTYN	And the silver –
SHANNY	And the trash compactor.
FISCHER	Trash compactor?
MARTYN	For the black market.
LINDSAY	You're making this up!
FISCHER	To get the house back!
MARTYN	Thank god they didn't kidnap those kids.
SHANNY	Two little girls!
MARTYN	And take them overseas as child prostitutes.
SHANNY	In Russia!
MARTYN	Or Bangkok, though I'm sure the food there is *excellent.*
LINDSAY	There were no kidnappers! No robbers! We checked with the police about the area. Fischer went down there and talked to them.
FISCHER	(*Pointing at* MARTYN *and* SHANNY.) That would have proved it!

LINDSAY   What?

FISCHER   That you're making all this up!

LINDSAY   (*To* FISCHER.) *"Would have"?*

FISCHER   That this area is *completely safe!*

LINDSAY   You didn't go?!

FISCHER   Too much to do at work –

LINDSAY   It was in your task column!

FISCHER   I know –

LINDSAY   Goddamnit!

FISCHER   I'll defend us here.

LINDSAY   (*Sarcastically.*) Right!

FISCHER   If someone breaks in –

LINDSAY   *Fischer.*

FISCHER   Whether it's one bad guy or a whole lacrosse
                   team.

LINDSAY   A what?

FISCHER   Buying you time to escape, or hide in the attic.

LINDSAY   The attic?!

FISCHER   So they can't find you –

LINDSAY   I am not Anne Frank.

FISCHER   Of course –

LINDSAY   *I am not Anne Frank!*

FISCHER   I know, I know – you're much prettier.

LINDSAY   (*To* MARTYN *and* SHANNY.) They're lying. They're
                 desperate and they're lying! They'll say
                 anything. Anything to keep this place now.
                 (*Scoffing.*) Asbestos!

                 (MARTYN *suddenly jumps up and exits.*)

FISCHER   (*At* MARTYN.) Hey!

LINDSAY   What did they think they were doing? We all sat
                 in that conference room and signed the papers.
                 There were documents and witnesses –

FISCHER   A big candy bowl.

LINDSAY   Right.

FISCHER   The fat receptionist brought it in.

SHANNY   Don't you mock fat people!

LINDSAY   Spare us.

SHANNY   It's not their fault!

LINDSAY   Oh, sure.

SHANNY   It's glandular.

LINDSAY   (*Pointing to her own neck.*) The chocolate gland!

SHANNY   I know lots of fat people and they're all
                 wonderful.

LINDSAY   At swallowing!

SHANNY   You'll be fat yourself one day!

LINDSAY   Never!

SHANNY   After all those kids you're so eager to have!
                Balloon right up. You'll see. Fat thighs. Saggy
                belly. Swollen feet. Bloated calves and floppy
                jowls and droopy, droopy grandma breasts!

FISCHER   (*To* LINDSAY.) Christ – tell me she's wrong.

                (MARTYN *charges back in. He's holding a big
                swathe of ripped asbestos piping insulation.*)

MARTYN   No asbestos, eh? Well, what do you call *this,*
                then?!

                (MARTYN *stands waving the swathe of asbestos
                insulation around in the air. As he does,
                asbestos dust goes flying everywhere.*)

MARTYN   From a pipe in the basement!

                (MARTYN *slaps the asbestos several times
                forcefully. More dust goes flying.*)

                Asbestos, buddy! Classic, classic asbestos! So
                don't you go calling us liars!

LINDSAY   The *rest* is lies –

MARTYN   You will not speak this way in our house!

FISCHER   *Our* house.

MARTYN   You will not insult us!

SHANNY   No.

MARTYN   Or mock us!

SHANNY   No!

MARTYN   Or accuse us!

LINDSAY   Or he'll make us *rinse!*

MARTYN   That's enough!

LINDSAY   We'll fix the sewer. We'll fix everything!

FISCHER   So it looks like something.

LINDSAY   (*Indicating house.*) Not like a big fungus!

MARTYN   (*Snapping and pointing at* LINDSAY.) Get out!

FISCHER   (*Pointing at* MARTYN.) Get out!

SHANNY   (*Pointing at* FISCHER.) Get out!

LINDSAY   (*Pointing at* SHANNY.) Get out!

                (*They all begin pointing at each other in a long,
                shifting Mexican standoff of pointing. Then
                there's a slow lowering of fingers. Then* LINDSAY
                *sits down possessively, as if sitting in her own
                living room. Then each one of them does the
                same. This is followed by a silent scene where
                each couple tries to outdo each other by acting
                possessively "naturally at home," as a way of
                claiming the house. This begins with normal
                behavior, then each couple tries to out-cuddle
                the other. These out-cuddle actions escalate
                to imitated sexual behavior. At some point,*
                LINDSAY *grabs the teddy bear and rubs it against
                her breasts, then crotch, then she and* FISCHER
                *have a threesome with it on the couch. After
                all this dies down,* FISCHER *and* LINDSAY *start an
                imaginary conversation from the future, as if
                sitting in the living room looking back in time.*)

FISCHER   Hey, honey.

LINDSAY   Yes, dear?

FISCHER   Remember when that dentist used to live here?

LINDSAY   (*Recalling.*) Oh, yeah, I remember him.

FISCHER	I was just thinking about him.
LINDSAY	He was sort of –
	(LINDSAY *makes a "wishy-washy" gesture with her hands.*)
FISCHER	Yep.
LINDSAY	But I guess they're like that, dentists.
FISCHER	Seems so.
LINDSAY	Just attracts the type.
FISCHER	(*Makes same hand gesture.*) This type.
LINDSAY	It's a little bit sad.
	(*Pause.*)
FISCHER	Knock, knock
LINDSAY	Who's there?
FISCHER	A dentist.
	(*Instead of replying,* LINDSAY *makes the hand gesture again. A pause as all four sit silently,* MARTYN *stewing. Then* MARTYN *speaks. His speech is "to the gods" rather than directly at* FISCHER *and* LINDSAY.)
MARTYN	(*Starting calmly, then building.*) Sure, go ahead and make fun of dentists. Go right ahead. Then remember that. Remember that after your daughter flips teeth-first over her handlebars. When you trip down the stairs after too many white-wine spritzers. Because when that nagging little tooth thing that's been bugging you starts turning sorer, then kinda painful-like, then sharper and sharper into a kind of shooting

zapping all around your face, because there's
a big infection in there now, a huge infection
in the pulp cavity that's burst out of the tooth
and into the bone, poisoning the marrow and
eating the tissue, growing and bubbling and
oozing and turning everything it touches *rancid*
as it get bigger and bigger, killing flesh faster
and faster, into your maxillary and malar and
ethmoid, spewing noxious gases inside your
skull, pressure building, your palate mortifying
and swelling and dropping into your mouth,
when your face starts blackening and bloating,
blood and pus bursting out of your eye sockets
– *you're gonna need a dentist!!!* So go ahead
and joke, laugh all you want. But we dentists
got *everything*. We got great houses and wives.
Our kids go to colleges covered in ivy and other
kinds of vines. We got classical music radio
stations perfect for root canals. We can look at
X-rays in ways that makes you really nervous.
We got drills the government wants to use on
terrorists. We get toothbrushes for free and our
cars are made in Bavaria! So remember that!
Remember that next time you insult a *Doctor of
Dental Surgery!*

(*A beat, then* LINDSAY *stands assertively, trying
to regain the upper hand, moving around as she
speaks.*)

LINDSAY   We'll have a housewarming party!

FISCHER   A huge one!

LINDSAY   We'll invite all the neighbors!

FISCHER   (*Looking around the living room, imagining the
               party.*) The room full up.

LINDSAY   (*Also imagining the party.*) The sound of hellos.

FISCHER   And laughter.

LINDSAY	Jazz from the stereo.
FISCHER	People mixing gin-and-tonics.
LINDSAY	Martinis.
FISCHER	Manhattans.
LINDSAY	The smell of vermouth!
FISCHER	Catering girls with trays.
LINDSAY	Serving shrimp cocktail.
FISCHER	Meatballs –
LINDSAY	Brie –
FISCHER	And things on sticks! We'll invite all the neighbors –
LINDSAY	They'll be *thrilled* the Redmonds are gone.
FISCHER	"Let the grass grow too long."
LINDSAY	"Put their trash out too early."
FISCHER	The greatest housewarming ever!
LINDSAY	In the greatest neighborhood ever.
FISCHER	With best guests in the greatest house ever!
SHANNY	(*Suddenly turning on* MARTYN *in anger.*) Moving was *your* idea!
MARTYN	You love that condo –
SHANNY	We could have stayed!
MARTYN	It was *both our* idea –
SHANNY	You thought it first!

MARTYN	You said yes!
SHANNY	You convinced me!
MARTYN	What?!
SHANNY	Like one of your patients –
MARTYN	Patients?
SHANNY	Talking them into crowns they don't need –
MARTYN	That was once!
SHANNY	Twice.
MARTYN	(*Acknowledging, but arguing.*) Twice! It has nothing to do with this –
SHANNY	(*Looking around in dismay.*) Our house!
MARTYN	Nothing to do with what we decided!
SHANNY	You said we had to move someday.
MARTYN	We do –
SHANNY	The house would get too big.
MARTYN	It will –
SHANNY	The stairs too risky. I'd rather stay and fall down them now. Fall down and break all my hips.
MARTYN	(*To* SHANNY.) You can't blame this all on me!
LINDSAY	(*To* MARTYN *and* SHANNY.) Maybe you'll like your condo –
SHANNY	(*To* LINDSAY.) You shut up! I'm sick of you! Sick of your clothes. Your law-firm hair-do. The way she sits – *there's something wrong with her anus!*

LINDSAY	There's nothing wrong with my anus!
FISCHER	Wha – ?
LINDSAY	(*To* FISCHER, *re. anus.*) Tell her! (*Pointing at* SHANNY, *scoffing.*) I should dress like her instead. Like someone at the shelter got to the *good donations* first!
SHANNY	My clothes?!
MARTYN	It's fine, I don't notice.
LINDSAY	(*Gesturing around room.*) And this room – she's not colorblind, she's pattern-blind!
SHANNY	(*Suddenly realizing.*) The height marks!
MARTYN	No!
SHANNY	They'll paint over the height marks!
LINDSAY	For *our kids'* heights.
MARTYN	Our family history!
FISCHER	But it's our turn now –
LINDSAY	You sold it.
MARTYN	(*Abruptly and desperate.*) The neighbors are black!
FISCHER	You said they were great!
MARTYN	They are, but they could turn any minute!
SHANNY	(*Sniffing wildly and dramatically.*) I smell radon!
MARTYN	(*To* FISCHER *and* LINDSAY, *re.* SHANNY.) Think what's gonna to happen to her! Old people snap! Change is too much for them. Forget to eat.

Stop bathing – she's going to smell *real bad,* thank you very much!

LINDSAY   She's outta here!

MARTYN   It'll be on your conscience.

SHANNY   They have no conscience!

FISCHER   We give to charity!

SHANNY   We give more!

LINDSAY   *We* do!

SHANNY   To soup kitchens.

MARTYN   The hospital.

LINDSAY   The symphony.

SHANNY   The museum.

FISCHER   Public radio.

MARTYN   The library.

LINDSAY   The theater.

SHANNY   The zoo.

MARTYN   To orphans.

LINDSAY   To *poorer* orphans!

MARTYN   Because we're *Episcopalians,* dammit!

SHANNY   We've got a Lord!

MARTYN   Who we pray to when we go to church most Sundays!

LINDSAY   It's not moral to lie about a house!

FISCHER   Or act so superior –

LINDSAY   (*Sarcastically.*) Maybe they are superior. Maybe
                   they're *completely* right! We should be bowing
                   down to them! Bowing to the volcano of their
                   righteousness!

                   (LINDSAY *has kneeled down on the floor.*)

LINDSAY   Down, Fischer! Down in supplication! To the
                   town's great gods of goodness!

                   (LINDSAY *lowers her face to the carpet.*)

LINDSAY   Take pity on us! Our sad unworthy lives!
                   Great, merciful Redmonds! Let the lava of your
                   goodness not destroy us!

                   (LINDSAY *leans back up. There are big brown
                   stains on her nose and forehead, which she is
                   unaware of.*)

LINDSAY   We must appease them!

                   (FISCHER *points at* LINDSAY'S *nose.* LINDSAY *stands
                   back up.*)

FISCHER   Honey –

LINDSAY   That's how they want it!

FISCHER   Lindsay –

                   (LINDSAY *is lost in her own anger, not hearing the
                   others.*)

SHANNY   (*To* MARTYN, *pointing at rug when* LINDSAY *was.*) I
                   thought you cleaned that!

                   (MARTYN *makes an "I tried" gesture.*)

LINDSAY   Thinking they're better than lawyers –

SHANNY	(*To* FISCHER.) The cat has diarrhea.
LINDSAY	Or business people –
FISCHER	*Diarrhea?!*
MARTYN	(*Defensively.*) Same color as the carpet!
LINDSAY	Than people who know how to make a better, better life!
	(LINDSAY *pauses, then sniffs the air.*)
LINDSAY	This house smells funny.
FISCHER	Lindsay, listen, you've got some –
LINDSAY	Nothing's going to smell funny when *we* live here. Because I know something about clean!
FISCHER	(*Pointing.*) Your nose, Lindsay –
LINDSAY	(*Defensively.*) Dr Bowman did a fine job.
FISCHER	(*Trying to correct.*) No –
LINDSAY	He did!
FISCHER	Look at it –
LINDSAY	I'm not going back!
FISCHER	That's not what –
LINDSAY	(*Re. her nose.*) I love it now!
FISCHER	Lindsay!
LINDSAY	It's perfect, now! Perfect!
SHANNY	(*To* LINDSAY, *straightforwardly.*) You have cat shit on your face.

                    (LINDSAY *pauses, then slowly raises her finger to her nose, wipes it across her nose, then holds her finger out and inspects it. She pauses. Then she turns and suddenly dives face-first into the couch, vigorously rubbing her face into the fabric to clean it.*)

LINDSAY   *Aaaahhhhhh!!!*

FISCHER   (*At* MARTYN *and* SHANNY.) You soiled my wife!

MARTYN   I'm sorry –

FISCHER   Who *are* you people?!

MARTYN   It was an accident –

FISCHER   (*Pointing to carpet.*) Who lives like this?

SHANNY   We don't –

FISCHER   (*To* MARTYN.) Is your office this dirty?!

MARTYN   Those patients could've caught hepatitis anywhere!

SHANNY   A public pool.

MARTYN   People don't know what they're leaking.

SHANNY   We're *hygienic*.

FISCHER   Tell that to my wife!

LINDSAY   (*Muffled.*) Aaah!

FISCHER   My wife with the fecal eye-liner! Where's that cat? I'll kill it, I'll kill it!

                    (FISCHER *grabs the asbestos swathe as a weapon to hit the cat with.*)

MARTYN	(*Shouting and gesturing around at the house.*) Hide, Bismarck, hide!
SHANNY	Run!
MARTYN	*Go, Bismarck, go!*
FISCHER	You call it *Bismarck?!*
SHANNY	Tommy named it –
MARTYN	He loves the History Channel –
FISCHER	It's *dead*, I swear it!
SHANNY	We need it for the mice.
FISCHER	(*Panicking in fear of mice.*) Mice?!
LINDSAY	(*Panicking at the cat shit.*) It's up my nose!

(FISCHER *jumps up onto the couch, afraid of mice, swinging the asbestos section at where he fears mice may be.* LINDSAY *is in a panic, trying to blow the cat shit out of her nose.* FISCHER *accidentally hits* MARTYN *with the asbestos,* MARTYN *then hits* FISCHER *back with a couch pillow, which commences a big fight between the couples. Couch cushions and pillows fly, their stuffing coming out. In anger,* LINDSAY *starts maniacally ripping the stuffing from the big teddy bear, hurling it at* SHANNY *and* MARTYN *and around the room. It's a big general melee that makes as big a mess as possible out of the living room set, feathers flying, furniture overturned, etc. This goes on for several moments, and then everyone collapses, exhausted and covered in the remnants of stuffing, feathers, pillows, etc. After a moment,* FISCHER *can be seen moving his mouth in a somewhat confused fashion. Slowly he reaches into his mouth, under his lip, and pulls out a tooth. He holds it up in front of himself, inspecting it.*)

FISCHER   I think this is that tooth of Shanny's.

(*MARTYN pats his shirt pocket, where he had put the tooth and discovers it's gone. FISCHER slowly passes the tooth over to MARTYN, who reaches out and takes it. MARTYN inspects it for a moment, nods in agreement, then reaches out and gently sets it atop the big molar on top of the bowling trophy. There's a moment of silence, then SHANNY, taking pity and with a combination of apology and sympathy, slowly picks up the towel and walks over to LINDSAY and hands it to her. LINDSAY accepts it and uses it to wipe her face and nose and mouth. MARTYN then pours her a drink and walks over and hands it to her.*)

LINDSAY   (*Weakly.*) Thanks.

(*MARTYN also pours SHANNY and FISCHER a drink and gives it to them. Then MARTYN gazes around the room, taking in his house, his home.*)

MARTYN   (*Calmly and reasonably to FISCHER and LINDSAY.*) Look – give it back to us. We'll return your money. This was all a mistake. We'll forget all this and keep it like it is. So the kids can come back for the holidays. Roasting Thanksgiving turkeys and singing Christmas carols at the neighbors.

LINDSAY   The Hindus?

MARTYN   The normal neighbors. This house is just who we are. We didn't realize.

(*Pause.*)

SHANNY   No. No, it's gone.

MARTYN	(*To* SHANNY.) We can get a lawyer. Joe Edwards – he's excellent if he hasn't been drinking.
SHANNY	It's gone. (*Pause.*) I made a cake.
MARTYN	(*Waving off the idea.*) No –
SHANNY	Earlier. To celebrate the sale.
	(SHANNY *gets up.*)
LINDSAY	That's not really nec –
SHANNY	I'll go get it.
	(SHANNY *exits, picking up the first-aid kit, antiseptic alcohol, and towel and takes them with her, to clean up a bit.* MARTYN, FISCHER, *and* LINDSAY *all remain, quiet and uncomfortable. After a moment,* FISCHER *speaks to break the awkward mood.*)
FISCHER	(*To* MARTYN.) Do you . . . do you have fillings yourself?
MARTYN	A few.
LINDSAY	I'm afraid of the dentist.
MARTYN	Yes, most people are.
LINDSAY	It's not the drilling. It's the waiting room. Too many . . . (*A really big shudder.*) . . . old magazines.
	(*They all fall silent again. After a lingering pause,* MARTYN *speaks.*)
MARTYN	(*To* FISCHER.) You must own a lot of stocks.
FISCHER	A fair amount.
MARTYN	I have a lot of municipal bond funds.

(FISCHER *sighs to himself about* MARTYN's *weak investment choice.*)

MARTYN   (*Concerned.*) Something . . . something wrong with those?

(FISCHER *is about to reply, then thinks better of it, then gives same sigh again. Another awkward pause among them all. Then* LINDSAY *speaks, trying to break this mood.*)

LINDSAY   (*To* MARTYN.) Do . . . do you have a favorite tooth?

(MARTYN *ponders a little, then shakes his head "no."* SHANNY *re-enters with the cake. It has several candles burning on top. She's a little out of it when she speaks.*)

SHANNY   Here we go –

FISCHER   The cake!

LINDSAY   Oh, it's a *lovely* cake.

MARTYN   Honey –

SHANNY   I baked it this morning.

LINDSAY   Oh, it wasn't necessary –

SHANNY   (*A bit flatly.*) The whole house smelled so good.

LINDSAY   (*Trying to be reassuring.*) I'll make cakes in there too.

SHANNY   It's hard for a kitchen to get used to new people, I think.

FISCHER   (*Re. cake.*) It looks good.

SHANNY	Hard for every room, really. It's so used to being one thing –
FISCHER	(*Re. cake.*) Tasty-looking.
SHANNY	Then it has to be another.
	(SHANNY *abruptly blows out the candles on the cake.*)
LINDSAY	I smell smoke.
MARTYN	It's the candles.
SHANNY	No.
MARTYN	Sure it is, you just blew them out.
FISCHER	(*Indicating his glass.*) It's that peat-y scotch.
SHANNY	No.
MARTYN	It's strong stuff.
SHANNY	No. (*Brief pause.*) No, it's the kitchen. (*Pause.*) And the den. (*Pause.*) And the back hall. (*Pause.*) They're on fire.
	(*Smoke starts to billow into the room from the direction of the kitchen.*)
SHANNY	All of them. I used the antiseptic alcohol and one of the candles.
LINDSAY	What?
	(*The low sounds of a fire can be heard.*)
SHANNY	Just splash the alcohol and touch the candle.
LINDSAY	No –
SHANNY	Then *whoosh* –

MARTYN   Shanny –

SHANNY   *Whoosh, whoosh, whoosh.*

LINDSAY   Smoke, Fischer –

MARTYN   Shanny!

SHANNY   So pretty, in its own way.

MARTYN   Shanny, what have you –

LINDSAY   It's a fire –

FISCHER   (*To* LINDSAY, *indicating direction of the front door.*) We need to get out –

LINDSAY   (*Gesturing accusatorily at* SHANNY.) You!

FISCHER   We need to get out of here!

SHANNY   Along the floor –

FISCHER   Lindsay!

SHANNY   Up the walls –

MARTYN   Shanny –

SHANNY   Then just everywhere.

LINDSAY   Our home!

SHANNY   That's right. *Your* home.

FISCHER   No!

LINDSAY   *No!*

SHANNY   Yes – yours now. All yours. (*Then with a smile and holding up the cake.*) Top *this* house warming!

(*Beat. Blackout.*

THE END

It should be clear from the staging that all four characters can escape, that no one will die in the fire.)